The children in a Montessori class are given the freedom that is the liberty of the human being, and this freedom allows the children to grow in social grace, inner discipline, and joy. These are the birthright of the human being who has been allowed to develop essential human qualities, and again Montessori teachers from all over the world could furnish examples of these. "Excuse me," said a child to a visitor commenting in a classroom that this was the Method where the children could do as they liked, "I do not know if we do as we like, but I know that we like what we do."

From the *Foreword*

D0050341

By Maria Montessori
Published by Ballantine Books:

THE DISCOVERY OF THE CHILD
THE SECRET OF CHILDHOOD

Books published by The Random House Publishing Group
are available at quantity discounts on bulk purchases for
premium, educational, fund-raising, and special sales use.
For details, please call 1-800-733-3000.

THE SECRET
OF CHILDHOOD

Maria Montessori

Translated by
M. Joseph Costelloe, S.J.
The Creighton University

BALLANTINE BOOKS • NEW YORK

A Ballantine Book
Published by The Random House Publishing Group

Copyright © 1966 by Fides Publishers, Inc.

Published in the United States by Ballantine Books, an imprint of The Random House Publishing Group, a division of Random House, Inc., New York, and simultaneously in Canada by Random House of Canada Limited, Toronto.

Ballantine and colophon are registered trademarks of Random House, Inc.

Cover Photo by David Seidman

ISBN 978-0-345-30583-1

This edition published by arrangement with Fides Publishers, Inc.

www.ballantinebooks.com

Printed in the United States of America

First Ballantine Books Edition: March 1972

42 41 40 39

Contents

PART III

Today's problems with regard to youth and childhood are the most patent proof that teaching is not the most important part of education. Yet the delusion persists that adults form the man through their teaching of the child.

Actually, education which consists mostly of direct teaching often impedes rather than helps natural human development. The early years are useless for the transmission of culture; therefore the first part of life is disregarded. But those apparently useless years are most fundamental, for during that period an astounding phenomenon takes place: the creation of a human psyche and the development of human behavior. The child learns to function independently, to manipulate, to walk, to talk, to think and to direct himself through his will. The process takes place not because adults teach but because the child creates.

The process remained mysterious until, aided by the intuition of one who loves truly, Dr. Maria Montessori penetrated into the hidden realm of the child's psyche and revealed it. The children who made this revelation possible came from the lowest strata of society; they were tearful, frightened and shy, yet greedy, violent, possessive and destructive. Gradually, as their psychic needs were fulfilled, they underwent such an extraordinary transformation that the press of the time wrote of "converted children." The witnessing of this spiritual phenomenon changed Dr. Montessori's life. It is true that the children learned writing spontaneously at four and a half years, but what was really important was their changed behavior. Man is not made of culture alone; there is something much more essential. If this part continues to be disregarded and emphasis put only on culture, the more advanced man becomes, the more dangerous he will be. Man has discovered flight, he has discovered atomic energy, but he has failed to discover himself.

Herein lies the real value of Dr. Montessori's contribution. To illustrate the radiance of the emerging souls of the children, she undertook a campaign that lasted all her life. After her death the Association Montessori Internationale continued her task with congresses and study conferences, by establishing Montessori societies and training courses. If children are to be given the aid they need, people must be trained. As time went on training centers were established in Ceylon, Denmark, England, Eire, France, Germany, India, Italy, Pakistan, Switzerland, and the United States. The people trained spread out to all continents, to the old and the new nations.

But Dr. Montessori's books remain the most effective instrument of the Association, and this first American translation of *The Secret of Childhood* is a very welcome addition indeed—for our work in all the English speaking countries, but especially in the United States. For here a number of schools use Montessori only as a teaching method. Here also, many people maintain that this is what Dr. Montessori meant. They disregard what she most valued: the contribution the child can give humanity. I have often thought this notion should be refuted because of the confusion it causes, but where can one find a person to speak with sufficient authority?

Here is the answer. Let Maria Montessori speak for herself.

Mario M. Montessori
Director General, Association Montessori Internationale
161 Koninginneweg-Amsterdam-Holland

On Januray 6, 1907, in a section of Rome noted and reported on for the crime, ignorance, illiteracy and poverty of its inhabitants, was begun a work that was to spread around the world. On this day in the midst of about fifty miserable children and a crowd of the notables of Rome, a doctor of medicine, a woman, the first in Italy, read from the Epistle for the Mass of the day, the Feast of the Epiphany—"Arise, shine; for thy light is come and the glory of the Lord is risen upon thee." As a conclusion, she added, "Perhaps it may be that this Children's Home may become a new Jerusalem, which, as it is multiplied among abandoned people, will bring light into education."

The newspapers criticized; Dr. Maria Montessori was asked what she meant by her speech, and she writes that she scarcely knew. She had first of all decided to study medicine in the face of great opposition—the year of her graduation was 1896. After graduation, she went to the Orthophrenic Clinic in Rome for further work with patients suffering from nervous and mental diseases. It was there that she became interested in the children; and after studying the work done with defectives by Itard and Séguin and spending some time in the Bourneville Clinic in Paris, she began, along with her medical work, to try to educate these children. After some time, she came to the conclusion that the defectives could be sent in for the normal examinations in Rome. When they passed these examinations, Dr. Montessori saw underneath the seeming miracle something of deeper significance. It was then that she began to see that there was a secret in the child which was being overlooked—a key to an unkown potential that was not being released. If the standard of the so-called "defective" children could approach that of the normal child, what was the matter with the education of normal children, that it could not produce better results? It was only some years later that she had a chance to work with normal children and then, in 1907, came the opening of the first *"Casa dei Bambini,"* the "Children's Home," in the San Lorenzo Quarter of Rome, that occasioned the outcry in the papers.

Now Montessori schools are in existence in many countries of the world; the "Montessori Method" has come back to America and Montessori has much notice, with both approval and disapproval, with interest and with skepticism, in many areas of American life. But along with genuine interest and combined with real desire to know, there is much confusion, uncertainty, misunderstanding and misconception, as to exactly what value Dr. Monstessori's work has for America and mankind today.

The magazines, journals, newspapers, educational reports, often carry a picture of Montessori that is half-true or incorrect. That is why it is of significance that *The Secret of Childhood* is being re-published, because within the title of this book lies the answer to the question of what Dr. Montessori attempted to do and the message that she tried to leave for mankind to read, in order that humanity should be enabled to understand her work in all its fullness. It is of importance that this re-publication has been done under the authorization of the Association Montessori Internationale.[1] This edition comes out with the sanction and approval of the organization founded in 1929 by Dr. Maria Montessori and Mr. Mario M. Montessori and which, in all the countries of the world where her work continues under the direction of the latter, is the one to whom recourse is had by those who wish to ensure that her work will not fail through their lack of standards.

The decision of Dr. Montessori to take up a career in medicine was eminently significant in view of her life's

[1] 161 Koninginneweg, Amsterdam, Holland

work, because this training for medicine formed in her a power of clinical, scientific observation which was to be the instrument she used during the rest of her life in her work for the children of the world. This work was not to start schools—Dr. Montessori did not wish what she set on foot to be called the "Method"—she said that she had not invented a process to be labelled with her name; she did not care for the world 'method' which denotes in our minds a system of schools and educational institutions. Over and over again, she insisted that we must think in terms of "help to life" if we were to understand what she was trying to make people see. If we are thinking of life, then, not of a school or class, we have to take a very much deeper, broader, and wider view than if we were to study merely a system of education. It is from this angle, therefore, the angle of the totality of Dr. Montessori's work, that we have to look if we are to understand what she meant by "the secret of childhood."

The first thing to do is to realize that Dr. Montessori was working for life, not merely for the educational process of life; and only if we understand this, can we begin to understand what was her real contribution to mankind. If we are studying life, not a child in a class, we are faced with something different from a person who has to be taught, someone who has to work at certain things for certain periods of time, someone who has to reproduce what has been assimilated, someone who will reach a certain standard of educational achievement, someone who will be granted a certain mark for work done, someone who will work and play well with others. This is not a child to be reported on, marked, graded, classified, labelled, but a living organism following a pattern of development. Life does not begin at three or whenever the child enters pre-school, nursery class, kindergarten or first grade. Life begins at the moment of conception, and at that moment we were faced with a cell so microscopic that it cannot be seen with the naked eye but which holds within itself all the potentialities of the human being it is to be.

How can we help this cell to fruition? Not at all by direct means—we cannot quicken its development; we cannot hasten the fully-developed embryo; we cannot change the pattern of the development of organs—this is the secret of embryonic growth. All we can do is by the indirect means of furnishing the necessities for the growth of the embryo and by keeping away obstacles which may hinder the eventual result. At the end of nine months, the child is born. He has the potentialities of the human being, but with little except his outward form to distinguish him from the young of animals. But all that he may become in later life is housed within the framework of the almost inert being that is all that we can see.

The child is a universal. He has existed in all ages and will continue to be born until the end of time. There is no child of pre-history, of the Middle Ages, no Victorian child, no modern child. There is, in reality, only the child, of all times, of all races, heir to tradition, hander-on of history, crucible of culture, pathway to peace. "The task of the child," said Dr. Montessori, "is to construct a man, orientated to his environment, adapted to his time, place, and culture." If we think of the child at birth and the child at three years of age, what an immense difference there is between them, what an enormous change has taken place. This is "the secret of childhood." What Dr. Montessori did was to demonstrate the existence of powers in the young child that appeared to have been unrecognized. What she strove for all her life was to aid the development of the child to the fullest possible realization of his individual potentialities. If Dr. Montessori's work is to be of help to the child of today, it can only be so in proportion to which the principles and values of the Montessori Method are held to and understood. What she did was to found a science of man, and like all sciences, the method of study rests upon a formula. Valid research as to whether or not Montessori is of value, and to what extent it is of value, to the American child of today, whether handicapped, underprivileged, overprivileged or normal, can only be carried out if the principles underlying Dr. Montessori's work are not tampered with and diluted, but understood and accepted in their entirety. One of the tasks of the national and international pedagogical committees of the Association Montessori Internationale is to make sure that research is continued but that the criteria are valid.

It is a pity that the criticisms levelled at Montessori from some quarters should be based upon apparent misinformation and misunderstanding. The method is rigid; it suppresses initiative; it promotes only neatness, order, and self-control; the method pushes the child too far in intellectual pursuits; there is no development of the imagination, no outlet for creativity. Anyone supported by the standards of the Association Montessori Internationale in their work in a Montessori school, realizes how far from being true is any one of these criticisms. As the "method" is based on the science of life, it cannot be rigid—this would contradict the premise on which it is built.

In whatever country a child may be born, he is endowed with what Dr. Montessori called "the absorbent mind."[1] This absorbent mind is of a form that is different from the mind of the adult. What grown-up, by dint of sitting almost silent for two years while a language unknown to him was spoken in his vicinity, could in a series of explosions produce the language in its entirety, with perfect pronunciation, completely correct grammar and syntax, and with all the intonation and nuances that are part of the speech of the native? Yet this is what children of two and a half are doing, all over the world.

This absorbent mind does not only take in language and reproduce it. It absorbs all that makes for the culture of the country and creates the native, the man of a particular time and place. Did the Frenchman learn to be French, the American, American, the Hindu, Hindu, after he entered school? The absorption of culture, of customs, of ideas, ideals, of sentiments, feelings, emotions, religion, take place during the period of the absorbent mind, in the child from zero to six. This quite obviously

[1] *The Absorbent Mind* was Dr. Montessori's last book on infant and early childhood development.

is going on all over the world. This is why the principle of the absorbent mind of the child is one of the most important in Dr. Montessori's work and one of the most highly criticized. No one pretends that it is harmful to allow the child to learn to speak his own language. Therefore, as the child has already engaged in a tremendous intellectual exercise, that of acquiring the ability to speak an unknown tongue, it surely cannot be harmful to allow him to continue to make use of his mind.

The child in a Montessori class is not pushed to intellectual accomplishment. What is opened out to him is the world, and he is given the keys to its exploration through the sensorial material which is an aid to the classification and organization of the impressions that his mind must already hold, unless the avenues of sense are blocked and unusable. It is the real world that we give to him, not the world of fantasy and make-believe, because it is in that real world that he is going to have to live, if the psychoanalyst's couch is not to be his end. How can one learn through group play what it means to be a mother, father, space pilot, dog, when one does not yet know what it means to be one's self?

Again, as Montessori is based on the study of life, it is pure creativity, as all life is creation. The child, like every other living organism, passes through successive stages of development, guided by what Dr. Montessori calls "sensitive periods." These sensitive periods are shown in children of all races, of all cultures, as the child is a universal living organism. During any particular sensitive period, the child shows an insatiable hunger for the acquisition of some particular knowledge or skill. This phenomenon has been demonstrated over and over again, in Montessori schools around the world. In the face of such a universal revelation, should the American child be deprived of the opportunity for the intellectual exploration that is going on in other continents? It is this intellectual exploration that forms the backbone and structure of all the creative work of the Montessori schools.

A small child, patiently repeating the taking out and replacing of knobbed cylinders into holes in a wooden black, and repeating over and over again, may appear at a cursory glance, to be an example of the rigid use to which the Montessori material is supposed to be put. Surely if the child were allowed some freer use of the apparatus, the repetition would not be necessary. But repetition of an exercise, without command or suggestion of an adult, is another of the phenomena that are commonplace in Montessori schools all over the world. To repeat is to acquire understanding, is to demonstrate concentration, is to show the power of the human intellect. In this instance, also, Dr. Montessori showed, in her acceptance of this phenomenon of repetition, how great was her understanding of the powers of the human person, as exhibited first of all by the children in 1907 and since then, in so many countries of the world.

The children in a Montessori class are given the freedom that is the liberty of the human being, and this freedom allows the children to grow in social grace, inner discipline, and joy. These are the birthright of the human being who has been allowed to develop essential human qualities, and again Montessori teachers from all over the world could furnish examples of these. "Excuse me," said a child to a visitor commenting in a classroom that this was the Method where the children could do as they liked, "I do not know if we do as we like, but I know that we like what we do."

The absorbent mind and its functioning, the sensitive periods of development, the importance of repetition, the need of the prepared environment, liberty leading to inner discipline, concentration, joy in work, social development —these principles of the Montessori Method have been shown to be universally applicable. It is because of the persistence of the phenomena shown by children all over the world, when these principles have been fully understood and applied, that Montessori schools continue to be set up in so many different countries, in spite of continued criticism and misunderstanding.

It is because the principles are applied to an individual, not to a class of children, that there is continual possibility of development for each child according to his own rhythm of progress and to his own individual potentiality. The principle underlying the Exercises of Practical Life is held to in Montessori schools because of the need that each child has to learn to function as an individual of a certain race and culture, but the particular exercises given vary with each country and environment. As all in the class are individuals, the interests vary, as well as the potential. No child is forced to follow the interests of others. Because of this, an infinite variety of opportunities for research and extension of work is evidenced in Montessori schools.

For example—the child of two and a half who had had a lesson on the solid geometric forms and next day at breakfast, took his egg in his hand and anounced that it was an ovoid; the child who had become interested in the corollas of flowers and went into the garden to pick as many different kinds as he could find and asked the teacher how he could "keep them forever" and was thus led to the new activity of drying the corollas; the children who were given a lesson in history on the Norman castle and who proceeded to make expeditions at the weekend to supplement by photographs, drawings, picture postcards, the material on architecture through the ages that they could find in the school and public library; the child, who, after a lesson on rainfall in England, came to say that she had discovered that there was a place in India which had as much rain in one day as any place in England had in a year and that she was going to make a study of the wettest and dryest places on the earth; the child, who, after repetition of the multiplication table of nine, went to show a visitor in the class that in the units the figures go from 9 to 0 and in the tens from 1 to 9; the child who brought a list of words and said that she had discovered that they had two functions, that of the noun and the verb, as one could ring the doorbell and wear a ring on one's finger.

These examples are to show that discovery takes place in all branches of knowledge—as the children are in an environment richly supplied with motives for activity, this material acts as a key to open the door to unlimited initiative on the part of the child. No child's mind is packed forcibly with items of knowledge but no child is restricted in the activity of his essentially human gift, that of the intellect of man.

It was through her power of acute observation of children, through her clinical and scientific approach to the living organism that was the object of her study, that Dr. Montessori, during her years of work with children, showed that in order to be able to help them in their task of the formation of man, we too must approach this study from a different viewpoint from that of those who think they know. Dr. Montessori pointed out to us, that if we are to help life, we have first of all to study it. Studying it, means that we do not try to teach it, we learn from it instead. We learn from this living organism, the child, its needs and tendencies. Only when we know the child's needs can we begin to learn how to cater for them.

In Chapter 6, "The Spiritual Embryo," Dr. Montessori says, "One of the great problems facing men is their failure to realize the fact that a child posesses an active psychic life even when he cannot manifest it, and that the child must secretly perfect this inner life over a long period of time."

She goes on:

We should regard this secret effort of the child as something sacred. We should welcome its arduous manifestations since it is in this creative period that an individuals future personality is determined.

This is why there must be a scientific study of the psychic needs of a child and why a suitable environment must be prepared for it.

We are now at the first stammerings of a science that must necessarily advance. Through it, if they but apply themselves, men will after great efforts come to know the secret of human development.

Dr. Montessori gives examples to show how greatly surprised she was over and over again by the revelations of the mind of the child. She tells of first realizing the sensitivity to tiny things, unnoticed by the adult, that is shown by children during their second year. There was the child of fifteen months, gazing down in wonder at the ground, where was moving very quickly, a tiny, almost invisible insect. And the child who, amid an abundance of pictures of all kinds, was interested only in the fact that a car could be made very tiny, in a far corner of a picture, and could be represented by a dot. Dr. Montessori speaks of "the enigmas of infancy." The manifestations of the spirit of the child were not drawn forth by Dr. Montessori. What was shown to her were the same revelations that must have occurred since the child first appeared on earth. Adults must have seen and heard and remained unaware, because the facts did not pierce their consciousness. The secret of development remained unknown until Dr. Montessori illustrated for us the deep spiritual meaning and significance of "the secret of childhood."

She prepared an environment in which impediments to development were removed and in which the child was set free to reveal his needs and tendencies. Dr. Montessori also attempted to train adults to search with her for the secret of childhood. It was within this prepared environment that "the first unexpected results found me amazed and often incredulous." Their feeling for order, the choice of tasks which appeared to correspond to their inner needs, their indifference to rewards and punishments, their understanding and love of silence, their sense of dignity, the spontaneous discipline, the explosion into writing and reading—the spread of Montessori schools then enabled Dr. Montessori to note that these features were constant, were universal tendencies, were "the *natural laws* which should form the first bases of education."

The secret of childhood is the secret of life itself—the creative force guiding the human organism from the moment of conception. In order to be initiated ourselves into this "secret," we have to be able to look at the child as someone who holds within himself the mystery that is the potential of every human being. To release this potential, to understand this mystery, to penetrate to the center of the wonder of life, we have to detach ourselves from our role as adults all-knowing and put on, Dr. Montessori says, "the vesture of humility." Only then shall we begin to understand that in order to penetrate the "secret of childhood," we have to be prepared for the mystery of life, the mystery of creation—that we are faced with an idea that is not our idea, a power that is not our power, a vision that is greater than anything we could conceive. Looking at the child, with eyes unclouded by adult prejudice, with a mind free from preconceived notions, we shall be able more and more fully to help the child to help himself.

This does not mean abandonment, this does not mean license, this does not mean passive observation; it entails true understanding of the task of the adult if we are to give the help that is inherent in Dr. Montessori's principles and practice. This help is not a mere allowance of free rein to all the activities of the developing human being—it is the help that consists in setting the child free to move along the path of normal human development, in allowing the nature of man to become strong and true. It is the help that, understanding the obstacles that may intrude into the child's path, best prevents this; and, after having understood the secret of childhood, the force and power of life, moving to the formation of the whole man of integrity and quality, the help that never stands in the way of this formation, is never wanting when needed, but is never over-assertive, never over-forced.

It is only the power of love that can enable the adult to come close enough to the child to understand him. Love and humility will unlock for us "the secret of childhood" and enable us to understand the inner significance and true meaning of Dr. Montessori's work.

Margaret E. Stephenson
Director of Training, Washington Montessori Institute, and Chairman of the AMI Pedagogical Committee in America.

INTRODUCTION

CHILDHOOD: A SOCIAL PROBLEM

For some years childhood has been an object of intense social interest. Like other great movements this interest has not been aroused by any single individual but it has burst forth like a volcano shooting forth fires in all directions. Science provided the incentive for this new movement by drastically reducing the rate of infant mortality. Then it came to be realized that children were frequently worn out from the drudgery of their school work.

Studies made of children's health showed that their lives were unhappy, their minds fatigued, their shoulders bent, and their chests so constricted that they easily fell prey to tuberculosis.

But now, after decades of research, we have come to see that children are human beings whose lives have been warped by those who have given them their life and sustenance and by the society of adults about them. But what are children? For adults, who are taken up with their own ever more absorbing occupations, they are a constant source of trouble. In the cramped quarters of modern cities, where families are crowded together, there is no real place for children. Certainly there is no place for them on the streets swarming with cars or on the sidewalks thronged with people hastening on their way. Adults have little time to spend on children since they are busy with their own pressing duties. Frequently both father and mother must work; and, if work is lacking, both they and their children endure great sufferings. Even when children live in more fortunate circumstances, they are

1

confined to their rooms and entrusted to the care of strangers. They may not pass into that part of the house reserved for their parents. There is no place where they feel that they are understood and where they can carry out their own proper activities. They must keep quiet and touch nothing, since nothing is their own. Everything is inviolable, the exclusive property of adults and, consequently, forbidden to children. What do they own? Nothing. Not too long ago small children did not even have their own little chairs to use.

When a child sat on the floor or on the furniture of his elders, he was scolded. Someone had to pick him up and hold him on his lap. And this still is the condition of a child who lives in adult surroundings. He is like a beggar that looks for something and fails to obtain it. When he enters a room he is immediately repulsed. His position is like that of one who has been robbed of his home and civil rights. He is a being relegated to the margins of society, to be condemned, insulted, and punished by any adult as if this were the latter's natural right.

Because of some psychological quirk, adults are little concerned with preparing a proper environment for their children. It might even be said that society is ashamed of them. Though men make laws for themselves, they have left their offspring without laws, and, consequently, outside of them. Children become the victims of the parents' tyrannical instincts. And yet children come into the world endowed with new energies that could correct the errors of past generations and give a new breath of life to the world.

In recent years, however, men, who for long centuries, perhaps even from the very beginning, were insensible to the needs and destiny of their children have become more aware of them. A great advance was made through child hygiene which saved vast numbers of infants from perishing in their first year of life. At the beginning of the twentieth century, when men began to take proper care of their health, the life of a child came to be seen under a new aspect. Schools were modernized. New principles of education characterized by their sweetness and tolerance were adopted in homes and schools.

In addition to these results, which may be attributed to the advancements made in science, there were other movements which had their origins in a deepening of human sensitivity. Children are now taken into account. In the cities, gardens are set aside for them and parks and squares are reserved for their games. Children's theaters have been created, and books and magazines are published especially for them. They have their own outings and furniture to fit their needs. With the growth in social consciousness, various efforts have been made to provide organizations such as the Boy Scouts or Campfire Girls which give the children training and a sense of their own dignity. Political agitators have also sought to gain possession of children in order to make them the docile instruments of their own revolutionary projects. Whether we like it or not, the interest now being taken in children is here to stay, whether it is directed towards their own good or whether it uses them as means to some further end. Childhood is now recognized as an essential part of society. Children are no longer the sole concern of their parents to be paraded around in their Sunday best. No, they are now recognized as a part of the society in which they live.

As we have already observed, the improved status of children has not been achieved through the efforts of individuals or even the cooperation of various groups and organizations. To what must it be ascribed? To the fact that the child's day has dawned. bringing with it consequences for society that are of the utmost importance.

We must evaluate the significance of this new development for society, for the state, and for the whole of humanity. The various spontaneous movements without any reciprocal ties that have given rise to this new interest in children show that it was not the result of any single factor but rather of a natural surge and impulse towards a great social reform, and one which heralds a new era. We are the last survivors of an epoch that is now passed, when men were solely occupied in creating an easy, comfortable, and adult existence for themselves without a real regard for children.

We now find ourselves on the threshhold of a new era when it will be necessary to work for both children and adults. We are entering now upon a new political order that must provide for its subjects two distinct social environments, one for the adult and one for the child.

The task that confronts us is not the further organization of social movements already begun or the coordination of various private enterprises on behalf of children, for in so doing we would simply be acting as adults banded together to assist something outside ourselves, children, without really coming to the heart of the problem.

Instead, the social question of childhood penetrates deeply into our inner lives, rousing our consciences and stirring us to act. A child is not a stranger, one simply to be observed from outside. Rather, childhood constitutes the most important element in an adult's life, for it is in his early years that a man is made.

The well-being of the adult is intimately connected with the kind of life that he had when he was a child. Our mistakes fall upon our children and make an indelible impression upon them. We shall die, but our children will suffer the consequences of our errors. Whatever affects a child affects humanity, for it is in the delicate and secret recesses of his soul that a man's education is accomplished.

Diligent and consciencious efforts made on behalf of children will enable us to discover the secrets of mankind just as scientific investigations have enabled us to penetrate into so many of the secrets of nature.

The social question of childhood might be compared to a tiny plant that has hardly broken through the earth but which attracts us by its freshness. Its roots are deep and not easy to remove. If we dig down and remove the dirt, we shall see that they extend like a labyrinth far out in all directions.

These roots are symbolic of man's obtuseness. We must

remove the accretions of years that prevent us from really understanding children and acquiring an intuitive knowledge of their souls.

The startling blindness of adults, their insensibility with regard to their own offspring, is something that is deeply rooted and of long duration. An adult who loves children but unconsciously condemns them inflicts upon them a secret sorrow which is a mirror of his own mistakes. The social question of childhood makes us appreciate the laws governing man's natural development. It gives us a new awareness of ourselves and a new direction to our social life.

PART I

1. THE ERA OF THE CHILD

The progress made in recent years in the care and education of children has been so amazingly rapid that it is more to be attributed to a general awakening of conscience than to a rise in the standard of living. First, there has been the progress made in the care of children's health, which had its rise in the last decade of the nineteenth century, and, second, there has been the new and highly important light that has been thrown on the child's personality itself.

Today it is impossible to study any branch of medicine, philosophy, or sociology without taking into account the contributions gained from the study of child life. This is much more important, for example, than the light which embryology has thrown on every phase of biology and evolution. But the influence of the knowledge to be derived from children is much greater in that it extends to all human questions.

It is not the child as a physical but as a psychic being that can provide a strong impetus to the betterment of mankind. It is the spirit of the child that can determine the course of human progress and lead it perhaps even to a higher form of civilization.

Ellen Key, a Swedish poet and author, actually foretold that our century would be *the century of the child*. A similar expression may be found in the first speech given by Victor Emmanuel III as king by those who have the patience to search through the records. In this address, delivered in 1900, on the very threshhold of the century, he referred to the new era opening up with the century, calling it "the century of childhood."

These prophetic utterances may well reflect the impressions aroused in men's minds by the science of the last decade of the nineteenth century, when they came to appreciate the sufferings endured by children from infectious diseases, which carried them off ten times as frequently as adults, and from the rigors of school.

But no one could have foreseen that children had concealed within themselves a vital secret capable of lifting the veil that covered the human soul, that they carried within themselves something which, if discovered, would help adults to solve their own individual and social problems. And it is this which can lay the foundation of a new science of child study that can have an important influence on the whole of society.

THE CHILD AND PSYCHOANALYSIS

Psychoanalysis has opened up a hitherto unknown field of research, enabling us to penetrate into the secrets of the subconscious, but it has solved very few of the urgent problems of practical life. Nevertheless it can help us understand the contributions that can be given by the hidden life of a child.

Psychoanalysis has, we may say, broken through what psychology once thought was impassable, the rind of consciousness, just as men finally passed through the Pillars of Hercules, which ancient thought once set as the limits of the world.

If psychoanalysis had not sounded the ocean of the subconscious, it would be difficult to explain how a child's mind could give us a deeper understanding of human problems.

As is well known, psychoanalysis was originally a branch of medicine, a new technique for the cure of psychic disorders. It made a truly brilliant discovery of the power which the subconscious has over the actions of men. It has revolutionized older ideas by penetrating into the subconscious and making a study of psychic reactions which bring to light secret factors of great importance. They reveal a vast and unknown world but one intimately connected with a person's destiny. But psychoanalysis has not succeeded in exploring this unknown world. It has hardly gone beyond the Pillars of Hercules and has not ventured out into the expanses of the ocean. A prejudice similar to that of the ancient Greeks limited Freud to the study of pathological rather than normal cases.

In the last century the psychiatrist Charcot discovered the subconscious. In exceptional cases of grave psychic illness the subconscious was seen to manifest itself like the inner seething of a volcano that breaks through the crust of the earth. The strange contrasts between the subconscious and the individual's conscious state were taken simply as symptoms of the disease. Freud advanced further. Making use of an elaborate technique he discovered a way to penetrate into the subconscious, but he was almost exclusively concerned with abnormal states. For how many normal individuals would freely submit themselves to the painful tests of psychoanalysis, that is, to a kind of operation on one's soul? It was from treating the sick that Freud deduced his psychological theories. The new psychology was, as a consequence, largely based on personal experiences in dealing with abnormal cases. Freud beheld the ocean, but he did not explore it, and he portrayed it as a stormy strait.

This is why Freud's theories are inadequate and why his technique for treating the mentally ill is not entirely satisfactory and does not always lead to a cure. And this is why social traditions, the deposit of ancient experiences, have set up barriers to some of Freud's theoretical generalizations. For the exploration of the immense reality of the subconscious, there is obviously a need for something more than clinical techniques and theoretical deductions.

THE SECRET OF CHILDHOOD

Other branches of science and different concepts should also be used to enter into this vast unexplored region of the subconscious. These can perhaps help us in our study of man from his origins as we seek to trace the development of a child's soul through its reaction to his environment and witness the tragic drama of the secret struggles which leave the soul dark and twisted.

One of the most striking discoveries of psychoanalysis was that a psychosis can have its origins in infancy. Forgotten incidents called up from the subconscious have shown that children were victims of unknown sufferings. This discovery was both impressive and disturbing since it was so opposed to what was generally believed. These childhood sufferings of a purely psychic order are slow and persistent, and they have never been recognized as potential causes of psychic illness in adults. They sprang from the *repressions* of a child's spontaneous activity by a dominating adult. They are consequently associated with the adult whose influence is greatest over the child, the child's mother.

We should carefully distinguish between two levels of inquiry open to psychoanalysis. One of these, which is more superficial, comes from the struggle between an individual's natural instincts and the environmental conditions to which he must adapt himself, since these are often in conflict with his primitive desires. Such conflicts can be cured since it is not difficult to bring the underlying causes of the disturbance to the level of consciousness. But there is another and deeper level that must at times be probed, that of childhood memories, where the conflict was not between a man and his current social environment but between a child and his mother, or, more generally, between a child and an adult.

Conflicts of this sort, which have scarcely been touched by psychoanalysis, are difficult to cure. Little has been done to resolve such conflicts; at best they have been taken as an indication of the cause of illness.

In the treatment of any disease, whether physical or mental, it is now recognized that what occurred in one's childhood should be taken into account. Those sicknesses that can be traced back to childhood are as a rule the most difficult to cure and the most serious. The reason for this is that the pattern of an adult's life is fixed in his early years.

Though physical ills have led to the development of special branches of medicine such as prenatal care and infant hygiene and have made society much more conscious of the physical health of children, men's mental ills have produced no similar effect. Though it is now realized that serious psychic disturbances in adults and their difficulties in adjusting themselves to the world in which they live have their origin in childhood, no attempts have been made to resolve these childhood conflicts.

Failure to do so may perhaps be due to the fact that psychoanalysis employs a technique of probing the subconscious. But this technique, which makes surprising discoveries in the case of adults, cannot be used with children and actually proves to be an obstacle if attempted. A child cannot be induced to recall something which happened in childhood since he is still in that state. Consequently, when dealing with children, there is greater need of observation than of probing. But this observation must be made from a psychic point of view and aim at discovering the conflicts that a child experiences in his relations with adults and his general social environment. It is obvious that such an approach leads us away from psychoanalytical theories and techniques into a new field of observation of a child and his social surroundings.

Such a procedure does not involve the difficult task of probing the ills of a diseased mind but of grasping the realities of human life as mirrored in the soul of a child. Practically speaking, it embraces the whole of human life from the time of birth. The history of the adventures of the human soul has yet to be written. No one has as yet described the obstacles which a child encounters or his conflicts with adults stronger than himself, who rule but fail to understand him. No one has portrayed a child's unknown sufferings, the turmoil to which his delicate soul is subjected, his failure to attain the goal intended by nature, and the growth within his subconscious self of an inferior man.

Psychoanalysis is here of little help since it is primarily concerned with diseases and remedial treatments. On the other hand, psychoanalysis can be helped by this study of the child's soul, since it deals with something that is normal and universal and aims at preventing the conflicts which are the cause of the mental diseases with which psychoanalysis is concerned.

A new field of scientific exploration has thus come into being about the child. Similar to, but distinct from, psychoanalysis, it is concerned with what is normal rather than what is abnormal and strives *to assist the psychic life of children*. It aims at furthering our knowledge of this life and awakening the consciences of adults whose erroneous attitudes towards children are the product of their own subconscious selves.

2. THE ACCUSED

"Repression," the term used by Freud to describe the deep-seated origins of psychic disturbances in an adult, is self-explanatory.

A child cannot develop and expand as it should because an adult "represses" it. But this word "adult" is in itself an abstract term. In reality a child is isolated from society; if an "adult" influences him, it is a specific adult, the adult closest to him. And ordinarily this would be first his mother, then his father, and finally his teacher.

Society, however, attributes to adults a completely different role: it credits them with the education and development of the child. But now, after the human soul has been probed to its depths, there rises from it an *accusation* against those formerly regarded as the guardians and benefactors of mankind. But since nearly all adults are either mothers, fathers, teachers, or guardians of children, we may say that all adults stand accused, that the society responsible for the welfare of children has been put on trial. There is something apocalyptic about this startling accusation; it is mysterious and terrible like the voice of the Last Judgment: "What have you done to the children I entrusted to you?"

The first reaction is one of protest and self-defense: "We did our best. We loved our children. We sacrificed ourselves for them." Two conflicting concepts are thus opposed to each other. One is conscious, the other rises up from the subconscious. The defense is familiar and deeply rooted, but of little interest to us here. What is of interest is the accusation and not the one who is accused. The latter wears himself out in the care and education of his

13

children; he finds himself embroiled in a labyrinth of problems. He is wandering, as it were, in an open forest but one without an exit, since he does not know that the cause of his wanderings, his errors, lies within himself.

All those who speak out on behalf of children should make this accusation against adults, and they should do so constantly and without exception.

Then, suddenly, this accusation becomes an object of keen interest, for it does not denounce unwitting errors, which would be humiliating, in as much as this would imply some personal failure, but *unconscious* errors. Such an accusation leads to self-knowledge and an increase in stature, for every true advance comes from a discovery and utilization of what was unknown.

This is why at all times men's attitudes toward their own errors have been contradictory. We are all pained by conscious error but attracted and fascinated by unknown error, for it is this type of error that holds the secret to progress beyond a known and desired goal and which can, as a consequence, raise us to a higher level. This is why a medieval knight, who was ready to fight over the least violation of his personal honor, could prostrate himself before the altar and humbly admit: "I am guilty; I declare it before all; it was my fault alone." Sacred Scripture furnishes us with some striking examples of these contrasting attitudes. Why did the crowds gather about Jonas at Nineveh, and why were they all, from king to commoner, so eager to join the throngs that encompassed him? He told them that they were such great sinners that if they were not converted, Nineveh would be destroyed. How did John the Baptist call the crowds to the banks of the Jordan? What charming titles did he find to produce such an unusual concourse of people. He called them all a "brood of vipers"!

Here indeed is a strange spiritual phenomenon: men rushing together to hear themselves accused. And, further, by thus coming together they assent to what is said and admit the error of their ways. Harsh and persistent accusations bring to the level of consciousness that which has lain buried in the subconscious. All spiritual development is a conquest of consciousness, which assumes to itself something that was formerly outside. It is by going along this road of discovery that civilization advances.

Now if a child is to be treated differently than he is today, if he is to be saved from the conflicts that endanger his psychic life, a radical change, and one upon which everything else will depend, must first be made; and this change must be made in the adult. Indeed, since the adult claims that he is doing all that he can for his child and, as he further declares, he is already sacrificing himself out of love for him, he acknowledges that he is confronted with an insurmountable problem. He must therefore have recourse to something that lies beyond his conscious and voluntary knowledge.

There is also much that is unknown about a child. There is a part of a child's soul that has always been unknown but which must be known. With a spirit of sacrifice and enthusiasm we must go in search like those who travel to foreign lands and tear up mountains in their search for hidden gold. This is what the adult must do who seeks the unknown factor that lies hidden in the depths of a child's soul. This is a labor in which all must share, without distinction of nation, race, or social standing since it means the bringing forth of an *indispensable element* for the moral progress of mankind.

Adults have not understood children or adolescents and they are, as a consequence, in continual conflict with them. The remedy is not that adults should gain some new intellectual knowledge or achieve a higher standard of culture. No, they must find a different point of departure. The adult must find within himself the still unknown error that prevents him from *seeing the child* as he is. If such a preparation is not made, if the attitudes relative to such a preparation are not acquired, he cannot go further.

The act of entering into oneself is not as difficult as is imagined, since error, even if it is unconscious, causes pain and suffering. A single hint of a remedy makes one feel an acute need for relief. A man who has a dislocated

finger longs to have it set since he knows that the pain will
not cease and he will not be able to use his hand till this is
done. In the same way, as soon as one realizes that he has
erred, he feels compelled to set himself in order since the
knowledge that he has acquired makes the weakness and
suffering that he has long endured unbearable. When order is established everything advances smoothly. As soon
as we are convinced that we have attributed too much to
ourselves and have believed that we could do what actually was beyond the limits of our strength, we are eager and
able to recognize the properties of souls so different from
our own as those of children.

In their dealings with children adults do not become
egotistic but egocentric. They look upon everything pertaining to a child's soul from their own point of view and,
consequently, their misapprehensions are constantly on the
increase. Because of this egocentric view, adults look upon
a child as *something empty* that is to be filled through
their own efforts, as *something inert and helpless* for
which they must do everything, as *something lacking an
inner guide* and in constant need of direction. In conclusion we may say that the adult looks upon himself as the
child's creator and judges the child's actions as good or
bad from the viewpoint of his own relations with the
child. The adult makes himself the touchstone of what is
good and evil in the child. He is infallible, the model upon
which the child must be molded. Any deviation on the
child's part from adult ways is regarded as an evil which
the adult hastens to correct.

An adult who acts in this way, even though he may be
convinced that he is filled with zeal, love, and a spirit of
sacrifice on behalf of his child, unconsciously suppresses
the development of *the child's own personality*.

3. BIOLOGICAL INTERLUDE

When K. F. Wolff published his findings on the division of germ cells he showed how living beings develop and grow, and at the same time he furnished us with a striking example of how inner forces work toward a predetermined goal. Through his experiments he thoroughly destroyed the physiological ideas of men like Leibnitz and Spallanzi, according to which a fertilized cell already contains the final form of the adult being. Philosophers of this period believed that a fertilized ovum contained in minute proportions, though imperfectly, the being that would eventually grow from it if it were placed in favorable surroundings. They came to this conclusion from examining the seeds of plants, which contain hidden between the two cotyledons a tiny plant with leaves and roots. If placed in the earth such a seed will grow and mature. And they transferred this notion to animals and men.

After the discovery of the microscope, however, Wolff was able to observe how living beings actually develop. He began with the embryos of birds and discovered that they originate in a single fertilized cell. The microscope showed that this cell does not possess the adult form, as had been previously imagined, but that it is like any other cell with a nucleus, protoplasm, and outer membrane. Further, every living being, whether plant or animal, comes eventually from such a primitive, undifferentiated cell. The tiny plant observed in seeds before the discovery of the microscope was in reality an embryo that had already developed from a primitive germ cell within the fruit and which would continue to grow once it had fallen to the ground.

17

The germ cell however differs from other cells in that it goes through a rapid process of division according to a predetermined plan, but there is not the least material evidence of this plan within the primitive cell itself, even though there are within it tiny bodies, the chromosones, that determine its hereditary characteristics.

If we were to trace the early development of an animal embryo we would see the original cell divide into two and then these two cells in turn divide into four, and this would continue until they formed a kind of empty sphere called the "morula." This sphere, as it develops, folds inwards so that another sphere with a double wall and open mouth is formed known as the "gastrula." By a continual process of cell division and involutions the embryo acquires a complexity of organs and sinews. The germ cell, therefore, which is without any visible design, follows the inner commands that it bears within itself. It is like a faithful servant who knows by heart a commission entrusted to him and carries it out without the help of any written documents which could betray the secret orders of his master. The inner plan can only be seen in the accomplished work of the indefatigable cells.

If the embryos of all mammals, and, consequently, in those of men as well, one of the first organs to appear is a tiny vesicle which develops into the heart. This beats with a fixed rhythm, twice as fast as the heartbeat of its mother. It provides the necessary sustenance for the living tissues which are being formed and beats and will continue to beat without becoming weary. The growth of the embryo is a miracle of creation and so wonderful because it is carried out in secret and alone. The cells make no mistakes in their extensive transformations. Some become cartilage, others nerves, others skin, and they all have their own separate functions to perform. This marvel of creation, however, has been carefully hidden. Nature has enveloped the growing embryo with impenetrable wrappings, and she alone breaks them when at the proper time she brings forth a new born creature into the world.

But the being that is born is something more than a

mere physical body. It is like the germ cell in that it has within itself predetermined psychic principles. Its body will not function merely through its various organs. It has instincts which are not to be found in the individual cells but within a living body. Just as every fertilized cell contains within itself the plan of the whole organism, so the body of a newborn creature, no matter to what species it may belong, has within itself psychic instincts which will enable it to adjust itself to its surroundings. This is true of every living being, even the humblest insect. The marvelous instincts of bees, which enable them to live and work in such a complex society, are not to be found in eggs or larvae but only in mature bees. A bird has an instinctive desire to fly only after it has been hatched, and so on.

When a new being comes into existence, it contains within itself mysterious guiding principles which will be the source of its work, character, and adaptation to its surroundings. The external environment in which an animal finds itself does not only provide it with the means for its physiological existence but it also furnishes stimuli for the special characteristics of each type of animal, and thus enable it to contribute in its own way to the general harmony and conservation of the world. Each species of animal has an environment best suited for it, and each species has its own peculiar bodily characteristics that enable it to contribute to the general economy of the world. The place an animal will have in the universe can be seen at birth. We know that one animal will be peaceful since it is a lamb, that another will be fierce because it is a lion cub, that one insect will toil without ceasing since it is an ant, and that another will do nothing but sing in solitude since it is a locust.

And just as the lower animals, so the newly born child has latent psychic drives characteristic of its species. It would be absurd to think that man alone, so superior to all other creatures in the grandeur of his psychic life, would be the only one to lack a plan of psychic development. Unlike the instincts of brute animals, which may be seen immediately in their way of acting, a child's spirit can be so deeply hidden that it is not immediately apparent. The very fact that it is not moved by the same type of predetermined instincts that are found in irrational creatures is an indication of the depth of its freedom of action. And this inner freedom requires a personal, secret, and difficult elaboration on the part of each individual. There is in the soul of a child an impenetrable secret that is gradually revealed as it develops. It is hidden like the pattern followed by the germ cell in its development which is only seen in the process of development.

This is why it is the child alone that can reveal the plan that is *natural* to man. But because of its delicate condition, like that of all incipient beings, the psychic life of a child needs to be protected and to be surrounded by an environment that could be compared with the wrappings placed by nature about the physical embryo.

4. THE NEWBORN CHILD

AN ALIEN ENVIRONMENT

At birth a child does not enter into a natural environment but into one that has already been extensively modified by men. It is an alien environment that has been built up at nature's expense by men in their desire to obtain for themselves an easier mode of existence.

But what care have men taken to assist the newborn child as it makes the most difficult adjustment of all, that of passing from one mode of existence to another? At no other period in his life does a man experience such a violent conflict and struggle, and consequent suffering, as at the time of birth. This is a period that certainly deserves to be seriously studied, but as yet no such study has been made.

Many believe that the world is much concerned with the newborn child.

But how?

When a child is born everyone is concerned about its mother. She has suffered. But has not the child suffered as well? Care is taken to shield the mother from light and noise. But what about the child who has come from a place where it was shielded from light and sound? It also has need of silence and darkness. It has grown in a place where it was protected from all assaults, from every change of temperature, in a fluid created for its rest. And in an instant it has changed this dark and silent home for the hostile air. Its tender body is exposed to the harsh contact of solid objects and is roughly handled by thoughtless adults.

21

The people of the house, it is true, hardly dare to touch the newborn infant because it is so fragile. They entrust it instead to expert hands. But all too often these hands are ill suited for so delicate a task. It is not enough that a child should be held firmly in strong hands; it must be handled properly. Before she is entrusted with the care of a sick or wounded adult, a nurse learns the proper way to move a patient, how to tie a bandage or apply a remedy without causing excessive pain.

But no such care is taken with regard to a newborn child. The doctor handles it without any particular regard, and when it starts to cry in desperation no one takes it seriously: those who hear it merely smile complacently. This is the way it speaks, and its cries enable it to cleanse its eyes and fill its lungs.

After birth the child is clothed at once. In earlier times it was tightly wrapped in bands, and the tiny body which had been folded within its mother's womb was stretched out immobile as if it were set in plaster. And yet clothes are not necessary for a newborn child, nor even during the first month of its existence. And, as a matter of fact, there has been a gradual evolution in this regard. The tight swaddling bands have disappeared and have given place to light garments; and, if the process is continued, the infant's wardrobe will completely disappear.

An infant should remain naked as it is so frequently represented in art. Since the child has lived within its mother's body, it has obvious need of being warmed, but its heat should come more from its surroundings than from its clothes, which do not actually provide warmth but only retain that which is already in the body. A proof of this may be seen in the way animals care for their young. Even though these may be covered with down or fur, their mothers still hover over them, warming them with their bodies.

There is no need to insist upon this lack of care for the newborn child. I am sure that if American parents could speak to me they would tell me of their concern for infants in America. German and English parents would also, I am certain, express surprise at my lack of knowledge of the progress that they have made in the care of children. Advances certainly have been made, as I know from personal experience in various countries, but still it must be said that nowhere is there found a sufficient awareness of what is really required by the newborn child.

If progress consists in seeing what has not been seen before and in doing what was once thought unnecessary or even impossible, we must confess that though much has been done for the newborn child, there is much more still to be done.

And here I might touch on one point: However much we may love a child, from the first moment of its arrival among us we are instinctively on our guard against it. With instinctive greed we hasten to protect whatever we possess even though it may have no intrinsic value. From the moment of a child's birth, the mind of an adult is dominated by this thought: "Take care that the infant does not soil anything or become a nuisance. Watch out! Be on your guard!"

I believe that when men will have acquired a better understanding of children they will find better means of caring for them. A newborn child should not simply be shielded from harm, but measures should also be taken to provide for psychic adjustment to the world about it. Experiments have shown the need of such provisions, and parents should be instructed in this regard.

Wealthy parents still provide magnificent cradles and precious lace for their children's clothes. But, by this standard, if whipping were still in fashion, they would see that it was done with a gold-handled switch. Such luxury shows complete ignorance of the psychic needs of a child. Family wealth should provide for a child's well-being and not for luxurious surroundings. Far better for a child would be a room shut off from the noises of the street, where there is peace and quiet, and where light and heat can be tempered and controlled.

Care also should be employed in lifting a child. This requires a certain amount of practice and skill. A newborn child is still weak. Like its mother it has passed through the danger of death. Unconsciously, the joy and satisfaction that we have in seeing it alive is in part a feeling of relief that a danger has been passed. Sometimes it may have difficulty in breathing and must be given oxygen, or it may be suffering from haemotoma, or bleeding under the skin. But still such a child must not be confused with an adult who is ill. The needs of a newborn child are not those of one who is sick but of one who is striving to adjust oneself physically and psychologically to new and strange surroundings.

Our attitude towards the newborn child should not be one of compassion but rather of reverence before the mystery of creation, that a spiritual being has been confined within limits perceptible to us.

I once saw a newborn infant that had been barely saved from suffocation plunged into a tub of water set upon the ground. As it was being swiftly lowered, the child opened wide its eyes, stretched out its tiny arms and legs, and gave a start as though it were falling. It was its first experience of fear.

The manner in which we touch and move a child, and the delicacy of feeling which should inspire us at the time, makes us think of the gestures that a priest uses at the altar. His hands are purified, his motions are studied and thoughtful, and his actions take place in silence and in darkness that is penetrated only by a light that has been softened in its passage through stained glass windows. A feeling of hope and elevation pervades the sacred place. It is in surroundings such as these that a newborn child should live.

If we make a comparison between the care given to a child and to its mother and try to imagine what it would be like for the mother to be treated as her child, we will see the error of our ways.

The mother is kept perfectly still, while her newborn baby is taken away so that it will not disturb her, and it is only brought back to be nursed. The infant is dressed in pretty clothes and tricked out in lace and ribbons and considerably shaken in the process. All this is equivalent to having the mother, immediately after the birth of her child, get up and dress for a reception.

The child is lifted from cradle to shoulder and again lowered as it is placed at its mother's side. Who would ever think of subjecting her to such exertions. The practice is justified by the claim that the child has no real consciousness and experiences neither pain nor pleasure. It would simply be foolish to treat a newborn child with too much care.

But what do we think of the care lavished on adults who are unconscious or in danger of death? It is the need of assistance and not the awareness of the need that demands the full attention of mind and feeling. There is really no justification for the way we treat infants.

The first period of human life has not been sufficiently explored, and yet we are constantly becoming more aware of its importance. Hardships and privations in the first months of a child's existence can, as we now know, influence the whole course of his future development. But if in the child are to be found the makings of the man, it is in the child also that the future welfare of the race is to be found.

Too little attention is paid to the newborn child that has just experienced the most difficult of human crises. When he appears in our midst, we hardly know how to receive him, even though he bears within himself a power to create a better world than that in which we live ourselves.

The words which we read in the prologue to St. John's Gospel are in a sense applicable to the newborn child: "He was in the world ... and the world knew him not. He came unto his own, and his own received him not."

5. THE NATURAL INSTINCTS

During the trying period of lactation, mammals are guided by instinct in the delicate care of their young. The lowly house cat provides us with an example of this solicitude in the way in which she hides her newborn kittens in some dark spot. She is so jealous of her offspring that she will not even let them be seen. But then, after a little time has passed, she leads them forth as beautiful and lively kittens.

An even greater care for their young is shown by animals living in a wild state. Most of these live in large flocks or herds; but the female, when she is about to give birth, withdraws from the company of her kind and seeks a hidden place apart. When she has brought forth her young, she keeps them isolated for two or three weeks, or even a month and more, the time varying according to the species. During this period the mother is nurse and helper to her offspring, shielding them from the light and noise that would disturb them by keeping them hidden in some quiet and sheltered spot. Although the young are usually born with their various powers fairly well developed, being able to stand and walk, their mother, with tender care, keeps them isolated until they have acquired greater strength and can adjust themselves to new surroundings. It is only then that she leads them to the rest of the flock so that they can live next to their kin.

The maternal instincts of these higher animals are all essentially alike, whether they be horses, bison, wild pigs, wolves, or tigers. And the way in which they manifest their concern for their young can be truly moving.

A female bison, after the birth of her calf, keeps it far from the herd for several weeks, all the while caring for it

26

with great tenderness. When the calf is cold, she covers it with her forelegs; when it is dirty, she patiently licks it clean; and when it is hungry, she stands on three legs instead of four so that it may nurse more easily. And after she has brought it to the herd, she continues to care for it with that patient indifference that is common to all female quadrupeds.

Some animals are not content with seeking a solitary place where their young may be born; they go to great pains to prepare a shelter for them. The female wolf, for example, looks for a cave in a dark and remote corner of a woods. But if she cannot find such a refuge, she digs a hole in the ground or finds a den in the hollow trunk of a tree which she lines with hair that she pulls from her breast. This not only provides warmth and protection for her cubs, but it also facilitates the nursing of her young, which are born, and remain for some time, with their eyes and ears closed. During this early period all females repel any attempts on the part of others to approach their young.

Among domestic animals these maternal instincts are at times deformed. Sows will even devour their own litters, whereas the female of the wild boar is one of the tenderest and most affectionate mothers. And lionesses, too, when caged in zoos, will eat their offspring. This would indicate that nature's protective instincts are rightly developed only when they are free from artificial constraints.

The maternal instinct in mammals plainly shows that their young have special need of assistance when they come into contact with their external environment. After the trial of birth and the simultaneous awakening of their various powers there is a critical period in which they have need of rest and seclusion. When this period has passed, they will still need months of care, feeding, and protection.

A mother animal is concerned not only with the bodily needs of her offspring but also with the development of its natural instincts, with the forming of another individual of the same species; and this takes place more effectively in a quiet and dimly lighted place. As its legs grow stronger, a foal learns to recognize and follow its mother and takes on a closer resemblance to a horse; but the mare will not allow anyone to approach her offspring until it has become a colt; and similarly, a cat will not allow her young to be examined until they have opened their eyes, have begun to walk, and have become, in a word, kittens.

Nature obviously watches over the growth of animals with the greatest care. As she strives to awaken the latent instincts of her offspring, the female shows her concern for something beyond their physical needs.

And, analogously, it may be said that over and above the delicate care that is lavished upon the physical wellfare of a newborn child, attention should be paid to its psychic needs as well.

6. THE SPIRITUAL EMBRYO

THE INCARNATION

One of the most profound mysteries of Christianity is the Incarnation, when "the Word was made flesh and dwelt among us." Something analogous to this mystery may be found in the birth of every child, when a spirit enclosed in flesh comes to live in the world.

Science prescinds from a child's "incarnation," and simply regards the newborn infant as a complex of organs and tissues that make up a living whole. And yet even this is a mystery. How could such a complicated living being ever have come into existence?

Special care should be shown for the psychic life of the newborn child. If it already has such a life at birth, how much greater will this be as it grows older? If we understand by "education" a child's psychic rather than its intellectual development, we may truly say, as it is said today, that a child's education should begin at birth.

Proof of a child's psychic life may be found in the distinction that is made between its conscious and its subconscious activities. But even if we limit ourselves to more obvious and basic concepts, we must admit that there is a play of instincts within a child not only with respect to its physical growth and nourishment but also with respect to various psychic operations. In brute animals such operations are characteristic of the species. As far as motion is concerned, a child develops more slowly than other animals. At birth this ability is little developed in a child even though he has the use of his senses and responds to light, touch, sound, and so forth.

A newborn baby is a pitiable sight. It is helpless and will remain so for a long time. It cannot speak; it cannot hold itself erect, it is in constant need of attention. For a long time the only sound that it will send forth is that of weeping or a cry that will cause others to rush to its assistance. Only after a considerable time, after months, a year, or even longer, will it be able to stand and walk. And it will be still longer before it can speak.

We can now describe a child's psychic and psysiological growth as a kind of "incarnation," understanding by this word that mysterious force which animates the helpless body of a newborn child. enables him to grow, teaches him to speak, and thus perfects him.

It is quite remarkable that a child remains helpless so long, whereas other young mammals almost immediately, or a short time after birth, can stand, walk, look for their dam, and have the language proper to their species, even though this is still imperfect and almost pathetic. Kittens have a real meow, lambs a timid bleating, and colts a plaintive neigh. Though they can be heard, they are more inclined to silence. The world is not, as a matter of fact, greatly disturbed by the cries and laments of newborn animals.

They grow quickly and without much trouble. The flesh of a newborn animal is already endowed with the instincts which will determine its later actions. We already know how a tiger cub will bound and how a kid that has as yet hardly stood upon its own four feet will jump. Every creature that is born has within itself instincts that transcend the functions of its psysiological organs. It manifests these in its activities, and they are more constant and distinctive of the species than the shape of the creature's body itself.

All the specific characteristics of an animal that are over and above its vegetative functions may be described as "psychic traits." Since such specific traits are found at birth in all animals, why should they not be found in a child as well?

There is a theory that explains the instincts of animals

as being the result of the accumulated experiences of the species in the past that have been continuously handed down as a kind of inheritance. Why are men so slow to inherit from their ancestors? They have always walked erect, have always spoken, and have always been inclined to provide for their descendants. It would be foolish to maintain that man alone, so superior to all other creatures in the richness of his psychic life, should be the only creature not to possess a pattern of psychic development.

There must be some hidden truth beneath this apparent contradiction. The human spirit can be so profoundly hidden that it does not readily reveal itself like the instinct of animals. The very fact that a child is not subject to fixed and predetermined guiding instincts is an indication of its innate liberty and freedom of action. This can perhaps be illustrated by a consideration of the different types of objects which men make for their own use. Many things are "mass produced," that is, they are turned out rapidly by machines and are all alike. Other objects are made by hand. They are produced slowly and each is different from the other. The merit of handmade objects is that each one of them bears the direct impress of its author. One reveals the skill of an embroiderer, another bears the stamp of genius of a great artist.

If we extend this comparison to living beings, we may say that the psychic difference between man and beast consists in the following: an animal is like an object that has been mass produced. Each individual possesses the special characteristics of its particular species. A man, on the other hand, is like an object turned out by hand. Each one is different from the other. Every man has his own creative spirit that makes him a work of art. But there is need of much toil and labor. Before any effects are outwardly apparent, an inner work must be performed which is not the simple reproduction of an already pre-existing type, but the active creation of a new type. The end product, when it does appear, is as a consequence something surprising and enigmatic. It is like a masterpiece which an artist has kept in the intimacy of his studio and into which he has poured himself before showing it in public.

This fashioning of the human personality is a secret work of "incarnation." The child is an enigma. All that we know is that he has the highest potentialities, but we do not know what he will be. He must "become incarnate" with the help of his own will.

That which is commonly called "flesh" is a complex of "voluntary muscles," which, as their name would indicate, are moved by the will. Without these muscles, so intimately connected with man's psychic life, the will could do nothing. Without some means of locomotion no living creature, even the lowliest insect, despite its instincts could move about. In the higher forms of life, and particularly in man, the muscles are so numerous and intricate that anatomists say a student has to go at least seven times through all the muscles before he can get to know them. These various muscles work together to carry out the most complicated kinds of activity. Some become active, others passive, sometimes they work together, and sometimes they work against each other.

An inhibition always accompanies a drive and corrects it. Many muscles will work in harmony together to perform the most complicated actions such as those of acrobats or of violin players, who can transfer their slightest movements to the bow. Every move and modulation requires the simultaneous action of innumerable components, each working to the perfection of the activity.

But men have never had complete confidence in nature since the guiding principle for human development is a personal energy contained within the child. The child's psychic life is independent of, precedes, and vitalizes every exterior activity.

It is a mistake to believe that a child is muscularly weak simply because it cannot stand or that it is naturally incapable of coordinating its movements. A newborn baby shows the strength of its muscles in the way it moves its limbs. Sucking and swallowing are complex operations involving a great deal of coordination of the muscles, and yet infants at birth, like other animals, can perform these actions. But in his other movements a child is left free by nature from the exacting demands of instincts. In the case of the child these are not predominant. The muscles, as they grow strong, await a command of the will to coordinate them. A child develops not simply as a member of the human species but as a person. We know that he will eventually speak and walk upright, but he will also manifest his own particular individuality.

We can readily know what young animals will be like when they mature. A gazelle will be light and swift of foot; an elephant will be awkward and heavy in its gait; a tiger will be fierce, and a rabbit will be a timid vegetarian.

But a man is capable of becoming anything, and his apparent helplessness as a child is the seedbed of his distinctive personality. The now inarticulate voice will one day speak, though in what language is yet unknown. This he will learn by paying attention to those about him, imitating the sounds he hears, first syllables and then words, to the best of his ability. Making use of his own will in his contact with his environment, he develops his various faculties and thus becomes in a sense his own creator.

Philosophers have always been intrigued with the state of a child so helpless after birth, but up to the present teachers and physicians have been too little concerned with it. Like many other things that lie hidden in the subconscious, the child's state has been considered simply as a fact without any particular significance.

In actual practice, however, such an attitude has endangered the psychic life of the child. It has led to the belief that not only are a child's muscles inactive but that the child himself is helpless, inactive, and without a psychic life of his own. Adults have consequently, though erroneously, believed that it is through their care and assistance that a child is so wonderful animated. They have looked upon such assistance as a personal responsibility and have imagined that they were the molders of the child and the builders of his psychic life. They imagine that they accomplish this creative work exteriorly by the directions and suggestions they give to the child to develop his feelings, intellect, and will.

In so doing, adults, claim for themselves an almost divine power, making themselves gods to their children, and applying to themselves the words of Genesis: "I will make man in my image." Pride was man's first sin; his attempts to replace God has been the cause of the misery of all his descendants.

But if a child has within himself the key to his own personality, if he has a plan of development and laws to be observed, these must be delicate powers indeed, and an adult by his untimely interventions can prevent their secret realization. From time immemorial men, through their interference with these natural laws, have hindered the divine plan for children and, as a consequence, God's plan for men themselves.

One of the great problems facing men is their failure to realize the fact that a child possesses an active psychic life even when he cannot manifest it, and that the child must secretly perfect this inner life over a long period of time.

The child is like a soul in a dark dungeon striving to come out into the light, to be born, to grow, and which slowly but surely animates the sluggish flesh, calling to it with the voice of its will. And, all the while, there is standing by a gigantic being of enormous power waiting to pounce upon it and crush it.

No preparations are made for this "incarnation" since there is no one who waits for it or even realizes what it is. Instead, it finds numerous obstacles in the way.

The child becoming incarnate is a spiritual embryo which needs its own special environment. Just as a physical embryo needs its mother's womb in which to grow, so the spiritual embryo needs to be protected by an external environment that is warm with love and rich in nourishment, where everything is disposed to welcome, and nothing to harm it.

When this is finally realized, adults will change their attitude towards children, for the image of a child as a spiritual being becoming incarnate not only stirs us but imposes upon us new responsibilities. As we look upon the charming little body, so much like a toy and upon which we lavish so much physical attention, we begin to appreciate the saying of the Roman poet, Juvenal: "The greatest reverence is owed to a child."

A child's incarnation is effected through hidden toil, and there is a drama about his creative efforts that has yet to be written.

No other creature experiences this tiring sensation of willing that which does not yet exist, of being obliged to give commands to inert faculties in order to make them active and disciplined. A delicate and uncertain life that is barely conscious makes contact with its environment through its senses and reaches out to it through its muscles in an unending attempt at self-realization.

There is an interchange between the individual, the spiritual embryo, and its environment. It is through the environment that the individual is molded and brought to perfection. A child is forced to come to terms with his surroundings and the efforts entailed lead to an integration of his personality.

This slow and gradual activity brings about a continuous conquest of the instrument by the spirit which must keep vigilant watch over its sovereignty so that its motions do not die from inertia or become mechanical. The spirit must be in constant command so that movements which are not under the direction of fixed instincts do not degenerate into chaos. The effort required to prevent this builds up its energies and contributes to the unending work of spiritual incarnation.

In this way, just as the embryo becomes a child and a child becomes a man, so the human personality is formed through its own efforts.

Actually, what do mother and father contribute to the life of their child? The father provides an invisible cell. In addition to another single cell, the mother provides a living environment for the fertilized ovum so that it can eventually grow into a fully developed child. It is not right to say that mother and father have made their child. Rather we should say: "The child is the father of the man."

We should regard this secret effort of the child as something sacred. We should welcome its arduous manifestations since it is in this creative period that an individual's future personality is determined.

This is why there must be a scientific study of the psychic needs of a child and why a suitable environment must be prepared for it.

We are now at the first stammerings of a science that must necessarily advance. Through it, if they but apply themselves, men will, after great efforts, come to know the secret of human development.

7. PSYCHIC DEVELOPMENT

THE SENSITIVE PERIODS

The sense perceptions of even the tiniest infants initiate their psychic development before there can be any question of its external expression.

Even though this development takes place in secret, it would be wrong to imagine, as in the case of speech, for example, that it is not happening. To take such an attitude would be the same as to say that a child already possesses in its soul the faculty of speech even though its external organs are as yet incapable of giving it proper expression. But what actually exists in the child is a predisposition for acquiring a language. And the same can be said of all the various aspects of his mental life. In an infant there is a creative instinct, an active potency for building up a psychic world at the expense of his environment.

In this regard, the discovery of the so-called "sensitive periods" that are closely connected with the phenomena of growth are of special interest.

When we speak of development and growth, we mean an exteriorly discernible fact. But the inner mechanism of growth has only recently been explored, and is still imperfectly understood. Modern science has furnished us with two means for attaining such knowledge. One of these consists in a study of the glands and internal secretions connected with physical growth. This has become popular because of its great importance for child health and care. The other consists in a study of the so-called "sensitive periods," which has led to an understanding of a child's mental growth.

The Dutch scientist Hugo de Vries discovered these sensitive periods in animals, but it was we, in our schools, who discovered that they are also to be found in children and can be used in teaching.

A sensitive period refers to a special sensibility which a creature acquires in its infantile state, while it is still in a process of evolution. It is a transient disposition and limited to the acquisition of a particular trait. Once this trait, or characteristic, has been acquired, the special sensibility disappears. Every specific characteristic of a living creature is thus attained through the help of a passing impulse or potency. Growth is therefore not to be attributed to a vague inherited predetermination but to efforts that are carefully guided by periodic, or transient, instincts. These give direction by furnishing an impulse towards a determined kind of activity that can differ notably from that of the adult of the species. De Vries first noticed the sensitive periods in insects. Their various metamorphoses represent various stages of development that are easily observable.

One example given by De Vries is that of the caterpillar of a common butterfly. We know that caterpillars grow rapidly and have a voracious appetite that is ruinous to plants. The particular caterpillar studied by De Vries was one which during the first days of its existence cannot feed on large leaves but only on the tender buds at the tips of the branches.

Like a good mother, the female butterfly instinctively lays her eggs in a sheltered spot at the angle formed by a branch with the trunk of the tree where they will be safe and sheltered. What will tell the tiny caterpillars when they break out of their shells that the tender leaves which they need for food are above them at the end of the branch? It is light! The caterpillar is extremely sensitive to light. Light attracts it, fascinates it, and as a consequence the tiny worm inches its way up to the end of the branch where there is the most light.

There among the tender leaves it finds the food to satisfy its ravenous hunger. The remarkable fact is that just as soon as the caterpillar has grown large enough to eat coarser food, its sensitive period passes and it loses its sensitivity to light. The instinct becomes dead and completely spent. It is no longer particularly attracted by light. The moment of usefulness of this sensitive period has passed, and the caterpillar goes along different paths in search of other experiences and other means of life. It is not that it has become blind but simply that it is henceforth indifferent to light. And this same larva, which has shown itself so voracious in eating, is in an instant changed by another active sensibility into a kind of fasting fakir. During its rigid fast it builds for itself a kind of sarcophagus in which it remains buried as if devoid of life; but it is actually intensely busy and emerges as an adult from its tomb equipped with wings and resplendent with beauty and light.

We know that the larvae of bees pass through a stage during which every female could become a queen. But the swarm chooses only one. The workers prepare for her a special food known as "bee bread." Fed on this royal diet, the chosen larva becomes the queen bee of the community. If the worker bees had chosen her when she was a trifle older she could not have become a queen, since she would have lost her fierce appetite and her body could not have developed into that of a queen.

Such illustrations should make us appreciate a crucial factor in the development of a child. There is within it a vital impulse which leads it to perform stupendous acts. Failure to follow out these impulses means that they become helpless and inept. Adults have no direct influence on these different states. But if a child has not been able to act according to the directives of his sensitive period, the opportunity of a natural conquest is lost, and is lost for good. During a psychic development a child makes truly miraculous conquests, and it is only our being accustomed to seeing this miracle under our eyes that makes us indifferent spectators. How does a child, starting with nothing, orient himself in this complicated world? How does he come to distinguish things, and by what marvelous means does he come to learn a language in all its minute details without a teacher but merely by living simply, joyfully, and without fatigue, whereas an adult has constant need of assistance to orient himself in a new environment and to learn a new language, which he finds tedious and which he will never master with that same perfection with which a child acquires his own mother tongue?

A child learns to adjust himself and make acquisitions in his sensitive periods. These are like a beam that lights interiorly or a battery that furnishes energy. It is this sensibility which enables a child to come into contact with the external world in a particularly intense manner. At such a time everything is easy; all is life and enthusiasm. Every effort marks an increase in power. Only when the goal has been obtained does fatigue and the weight of indifference come on.

When one of these psychic passions is exhausted, another is enkindled. Childhood thus passes from conquest to conquest in a constant rhythm that constitutes its joy and happiness. It is within this fair fire of the soul, which burns without consuming, that the creative work of man's spiritual world is brought to completion. On the other hand, when the sensitive period has disappeared, intellectual victories are reported through reasoning processes, voluntary efforts, and the toil of research. And from the torpor of indifference is born the weariness of labor. This then is the essential difference between the psychology of a child and that of an adult. A child has a special interior vitality which accounts for the miraculous manner in which he makes his natural conquests; but if during his sensitive stage a child is confronted with an obstacle to his toil, he suffers a disturbance or even warping of his being, a spiritual martyrdom that is still too little known, but whose scars are borne unconsciously by most adults.

Up till now we have not suspected this kind of growth, that is to say, the attainment of these specific characteristics; and yet through long experience we have noticed the sad and violent reactions of children when their vital activities are checked by external obstacles. Since the cause of such reactions was unknown, they were thought to be without any real basis and were simply measured by the resistance a child showed to our attempts to calm him. The name "whim," "caprice," or "tantrum" has been given to various phenomena that really have little in common. We regard as a caprice anything that does not have an apparent cause, any stubborn or unreasonable action. We have also noticed that certain types of tantrums can become aggravated. This in itself indicates a cause which continues to exercise its influence, and for which, obviously, a remedy has yet to be found.

The sensitive periods can throw much light on these childish tantrums, but not on all of them since there are different reasons behind inner conflicts, and a great deal of capricious activity is the result of deviations in the past that are only aggravated by wrong treatment. The various whims connected with the inner conflicts of the sensitive periods are transient like the sensitive periods themselves. They leave no permanent impress on the dispositions acquired in the sensitive period, but they can have a harmful effect in that they prevent one from ever attaining psychic maturity.

The tantrums of the sensitive periods are external manifestations of an unsatisfied need, expressions of alarm over a danger, or of something being out of place. They disappear just as soon as there is a possibility of satisfying the need or of eliminating the danger. One can at times observe in a child a sudden calm following a state of agitation that seemed almost pathological. We must, therefore, look for the cause behind every childish caprice, simply because this is what escapes our knowledge. When it is found, it enables us to penetrate into the mysterious recesses of the child's soul and provide the basis for an understanding of, and peace with, the child.

EXAMINING THE SENSITIVE PERIODS

The study of the "incarnation" of the child and of the sensitive periods might be compared to an exploratory operation which enables us to see the functioning of the various organs that promote the growth of the child. They show us that a child's psychic development does not take place by chance, that it does not originate in external stimuli but is guided by transient sensibilities, that is, by temporary instincts intimately connected with the acquisition of specific traits. Although this takes place within an external environment, the environment itself is more of an occasion than a cause: it simply provides the necessary means for spiritual growth, just as a material environment provides food and air for the development of the body.

A child's different inner sensibilities enable him to choose from his complex environment what is suitable and necessary for his growth. They make the child sensitive to some things, but leave him indifferent to others. When a particular sensitiveness is aroused in a child, it is like a light that shines on some objects but not on others, making of them his whole world. It is not simply a question of having an intense desire for certain situations or certain things. Within the child there is a unique potentiality for using these objects for his own growth, since it is during the sensitive period that he makes his psychic adjustments like that of being able to adapt himself to his environment or to move about with ever increasing ease and precision.

In this sensitive relationship between a child and his surroundings may be found the means for untangling the raveled skein of mystery that surrounds the spiritual growth of a child in all its wonders.

We might picture to ourselves this wonderful creative activity as a series of lively emotions rising up from the subconscious which, when they come into contact with their environment, build up one's consciousness. They begin in confusion and then move on to the making of distinctions and, ultimately, to creative activity, as may be seen, for example, in the way a child learns to speak.

As different sounds play chaotically about a child's ears they are suddenly and distinctly heard as something charming and attractive, like the sounds of an unknown language clearly pronounced. The soul which is still without thought hears a kind of music that fills its world. The child is moved to his very fibers, not, it is true, to all of them, but to those that have lain hidden and have till now only vibrated in fitful cries. They are aroused to a regular motion, and given an order and command that changes their manner of vibrating. This marks the beginning of a new period of life for the spiritual embryo. It is a life concentrated upon the present. The future glory of the being remains unknown.

Little by little the ears pick out various sounds and the child's tongue begins to move with a new animation. Before this the tongue had only been used for sucking. Now the child begins to experience inner vibrations. He feels out his throat, cheeks, and lips, while being driven on as it were by an irresistible impulse. As yet these vibrations serve no purpose except to give an unspeakable satisfaction. The child manifests the pleasure that he receives when he contracts his limbs, clenches his fists, lifts up his head, and turns toward one who is speaking and fixes his eyes intently upon his lips.

The child is passing through a sensitive period: a divine command is breathing upon this helpless being and animating it with its spirit. This inner drama of the child is a drama of love. It is a great reality unfolding within the secret areas of his soul and at times completely absorbing it. These marvelous activities wrought in humble silence cannot take place without leaving behind ennobling qualities that will accompany the child through life.

All this happens quietly and unnoticed as long as the child's environment adequately corresponds to his inner needs. In the acquirement of speech, for example, which is one of the most difficult of his attainments, a child's sensitive period remains unnoticed since he is surrounded by people who through their speech provide the necessary elements for his development. The only thing that can make us appreciate the sensitive state of the child is his smile, the joy he manifests when he is addressed in short words clearly spoken, so that he can distinguish the various sounds as one marks the tolling of bells in a cathedral tower. Or again it is apparent when we see a child grow calm from the bliss he experiences at evening when an adult sings him a lullaby, repeating again and again the same words. In the midst of such pleasure he leaves the world of consciousness to enter that of sleep. This is why we speak to a child in tender words. We wish to receive in reply his smile so full of life. And this is why from time immemorial parents have in the evening gone to their children who are eagerly looking for a song or story.

Such then are the positive proofs of a child's creative sensibilities. But there are also other, much more obvious, though negative proofs, of it. These become manifest when some obstacle impedes a child's inner functioning. A sensitive period can then reveal itself in the child's violent reaction. We look upon this as a kind of senseless desperation calling it a "tantrum." But in reality it is the expression of an inner disturbance or of an unsatisfied need that has created a degree of tension. It represents an effort of the soul to ask a question or to defend itself.

A tantrum can show itself in agitated and aimless movements. It may be compared with the high fevers which can suddenly attack a child without a proportionate pathological reason. As we know, it is quite common for a child to run an alarmingly high temperature for slight ills that would leave an adult practically undisturbed; but a child's fever can disappear as easily as it comes. Similarly, at the psychic level, there can be a violent agitation rising from a child's exceptional sensibility without a proportionate external cause. Such reactions have always been noted. In fact, the whims or tantrums that a child manifests almost from birth have been taken as proofs of the perversity of the human race; and yet, if every functional disturbance is considered as a functional sickness, we must also call psychic disturbances functional sicknesses. A child's first tantrums are the first ills of his soul.

Men have noted these tantrums, for pathological states are more apparent than natural ones. It is never peace that poses a problem and demands reflection, but trouble and disorder. It is not nature's laws but the deviations from her laws that are most obvious. Thus it is that no one notices the hardly perceptible external signs that accompany life's creative work or the operations that preserve it. Both creation and conservation remain hidden.

The same thing happens to living things that happens to the objects which men make. They are put under glass when finished, but the shops which produce them are closed to the public even though these latter are more interesting than the products themselves. In like fashion the operations of the various organs working within the body are truly wonderful, but no one sees or adverts to them. Even the person who is kept alive by the functioning of these organs is unaware of their stupendous complexity. Nature works without revealing herself. She carries out, as it were, the precept of Christian charity: "Let not your right hand know what your left is doing." The harmonious balance of the various forces at work is called "health" or "normality."

We take note of all the details of a disease and yet make no account of the marvels of health. Diseases have been known and treated from earliest times. Prehistoric men knew how to perform surgical operations as is evidenced from skeletal remains. The Egyptians and Greeks introduced the practice of medicine, but knowledge of the functions of the inner organs is comparatively recent. The discovery of the circulation of the blood goes back only to the seventeenth century. The first anatomical dissection of the human body occurred in 1600. It was the interest in pathology, in diseases, that gradually, though indirectly, led to the discovery and appreciation of the secrets of physiology, that is, of normal functions.

It should not then be surprising that the psychic ills of children have been emphasized while their normal operations have been buried in obscurity. And this is all the more understandable when we consider the extreme delicacy of the psychic functions, which gradually perfect themselves in secret darkness.

If no help is given to a child, if his environment is neglected, his psychic life will be in constant danger. A child is like a foundling in the world. He is exposed to harm. He must struggle for his psychic development and may fail in the contest. Adults do not help since they do not even know the forces at play. Much less are they aware of the miracle that is taking place, the creation of a psychic life from what is apparently nothing.

We can no longer remain blind to the psychic development of the child. We must assist him from his earliest moments. Such assistance will not consist in forming the child since this task belongs to nature herself, but in a delicate respect for the outward manifestations of this development and in providing those means necessary for his formation which he cannot obtain by his own efforts alone.

And if this is so, if the secret of a healthy child lies in some hidden energies, we can only imagine the great number of maladjustments which rise as a result of a defective psychic development consequent to functional disorders or ills. When the principles of infant hygiene were as yet unknown, the death rate of children was extraordinarily high, but this was only one aspect of the problem. Among those who survived there were many afflicted with blindness and rickets, or who were lame and paralyzed. Many had serious bodily defects and organic weaknesses that made them suspectible to infectious diseases such as tuberculosis, leprosy, and scrofula.

Similarly, we have no plan that guarantees the psychic health of the child. There is nothing in our own environment to protect and preserve it. We are even ignorant of the secret operations which enkindle the desire to create a spiritual harmony. Disorder causes numerous deformities —blindness, weakness, stunted growth, death itself, not to mention pride, the lust for power, avarice, and anger. All this is not simply a figure of speech or allegory but the terrible reality of a child's spiritual state described in the same terms as those just mentioned for his body. Slight errors at the beginning can cause the greatest deviations in later life. A man can grow and reach maturity within a spiritual environment that is really not his own. He lives shut out from the paradise that should have been his.

OBSERVATIONS AND EXAMPLES

Psychologists have attempted to elicit motor reactions from children which would indicate a psychic response to sensory stimuli. But such experiments cannot prove the existence of psychic life in tiny infants. A psychic life, even though it is rudimentary, must exist prior to any kind of voluntary movement.

A feeling provides the first impulse. Thus, for example, as Levine has shown with moving pictures, a child that wants an object stretches out his whole body for it. Only later with the progressive development and coordination of movement will he be able to isolate his various activities and reach out his hand for the desired object.

Another example of this may be seen in a four-month-old child that keeps his eyes fixed upon the lips of an adult who is speaking. By the movement of his own lips and especially by the fixed attitude of his head, the child shows that he is attracted by the person's voice. At six months a child can form a few separate syllables. But before he can utter these sounds he has listened attentively and secretly animated his organs of speech. This shows that he possesses a psychic principle that will animate his acts. The existence of such a sensibility may be known from observation but not from experiment. Psychological experiments at this early age would only prejudice the secret labor of the infant's psychic life by making too great a drain upon his energies.

The psychic life of a child must be observed in the same way that Fabre made his observations of insects. He kept himself concealed so as not to disturb them as they were busy about their work in their natural environment. We should start observing the child when his senses begin to accumulate conscious impressions of the external world, since it is then that a life is spontaneously developing at the expense of its environment.

One who would assist a child does not need to have recourse to elaborate observations or fancy interpretations. One must simply have the desire to help the child and a fund of common sense.

A few obvious examples will show how simple this observation can be. Since a child cannot stand, many maintain that he should always be stretched out. A child must receive his first sensible impressions from his surroundings, that is, from the heavens as well as from the earth, but he is not permitted to gaze at the sky. He contemplates the ceiling of his room, which is usually as white and monotonous as the cover of his bed. And yet he should have an opportunity to see those things which would nourish his thirsty spirit. Parents are frequently convinced that a child needs something to distract him from the sameness of his surroundings. Consequently, they tie a ball or some other object to a string and make it swing over the child's head. In his eagerness to absorb images from the environment, the child, who cannot as yet move his head, follows the oscillating object with his eyes. Because of the artificial position in which he is placed and the movement of the object, his efforts are unnatural and crippling.

Much better would be to place a child on a slightly inclined plane so that he could take in the whole of his surroundings. Better still would it be to place the child in a garden where he could see birds and flowers and gently swaying plants.

A child should be placed in the same spot on different occasions. He can thus repeatedly see the same things and learn how to recognize them and their relative positions and how to distinguish animate from inanimate objects.

8. ORDER

A very important and mysterious period is the one which makes a child extremely sensitive to order. This sensitiveness appears in a child's first year and continues on through the second. It may seem to us slightly fantastic that children should have a sensitive period with respect to external order, since it is a common opinion that children are disorderly by their very nature.

When a child lives in a city, in a closed environment full of various objects which adults move around and arrange for reasons which he does not understand, it is difficult to form a judgment about such a delicate attitude in the child. If he passes through a period sensitive to order, the disorder he perceives can be an obstacle to his development and a cause of abnormalities.

The soul of an infant has secret depths that are still unknown to the adults who care for him. How often does a child weep without apparent reason and resist all attempts to console him? This in itself should be sufficient reason to make us suspect that he has some secret need which must be satisfied.

A child's sensitiveness to order may be noticed even in the first months of his existence. A positive manifestation of it may be seen in the enthusiasm and joy which children who at seeing things in their proper places. Those who have been trained to observe according to our principles can easily recognize this. I can cite the example of a nurse who noticed that an infant girl in her charge showed delight and interest at seeing a white marble stone cemented into an ancient grey wall. Although the child was only five months old and her parents' villa was filled with

49

beautiful flowers, the nurse would every day stop the carriage in which she was pushing the child before this particular stone since it seemed to give such a lasting pleasure to the child.

But the presence of this sensitive period is perhaps more clearly shown by the obstacles that a child encounters, and it may well be that most childish tantrums are due to this sensibility. I can recall a number of examples of this. In one such instance the principal character was a little girl about six months old. One day she saw a woman enter the room where she happened to be and place her parasol upon the table. The child became agitated, not at the woman but at the umbrella, since after looking at it for some time she began to cry. The woman thinking that she wanted the parasol picked it up and brought it to her with a pleasant smile. But the infant pushed it away and continued to scream. Efforts were made to calm the child, but to no avail. She only became more agitated. What could be done to solve the tantrum? Suddenly the mother of the child through some psychological insight took the umbrella from the table and carried it into another room. The child immediately grew calm. The cause of her disturbance was the umbrella on the table. An object out of place had violently upset the little girl's pattern of memory as to how objects should be arranged.

Another example is that of a somewhat older child. I once found myself with a small group of tourists going through the tunnel of the Grotto of Nero at Naples. A young woman was leading a child of about a year and a half who was really too small to be able to negotiate the rather long trip on foot.

After some time the child became tired and his mother took him into her arms, but she had miscalculated her own strength. Her exertions made her warm, she stopped, removed her coat and hung it over her arm, and thus unencumbered she again picked up her child. But he began to cry, and his wailing became louder and louder. His mother tried in vain to calm him. She was obviously exhausted and became quite agitated herself. The other members of the group became uneasy and naturally offered their assistance. The child was passed from arm to arm but became ever more upset. Everyone was shouting encouragement, but this only worsened the situation. Apparently the child's mother would have to take him back. But by this time he had become frantic. It looked like a desperate situation.

Here the guide intervened and resolutely seized the child in his arms. Then a truly violent reaction set in on the part of the child. Since I was convinced that such reactions have a psychological basis in a child's inner sensibility, I decided to try something. I went up to the child's mother and said to her, "May I help you put on your coat?" She looked at me in surprise since she was still warm; but, confused, she yielded to my request and let me help her with her coat. The child immediately calmed down. As his tears and agitation disappeared he kept saying, "Coat ... shoulder," which meant, "Your coat is on your shoulders." Yes, mother should have her coat on her shoulders, which seemed to imply, "You have finally understood me." He stretched his arms out to his mother with a smile. We finished our journey through the tunnel without any further difficulties. A coat is made to be worn on the shoulders and should not hang like a rag on one's arm. The disorder he had noticed in the person of his mother had been the cause of a trying conflict.

Another family scene which I once witnessed is also highly significant. A woman who felt somewhat indisposed was lying back in an armchair propped up on two pillows. Her infant daughter, who was hardly twenty months old, came up to her and asked her for a "story." What mother can resist such a request? Though she did not feel well, the woman began to tell a little story which the child followed with the greatest attention. But her mother was so ill that she could not continue. She had to ask the maid to help her to bed in the next room. The little girl, who had been left behind near the chair, began to cry. It appeared obvious that she was weeping for her mother's sufferings, and those who were about her tried to calm her. When the maid began to take the pillows from the chair to carry them into the bedroom, the child began to cry out, "No, not the cushions . . . " It seemed as if she were trying to say, "Leave at least something in its place."

With soft words and caresses the child was brought to her mother's bed and the latter, despite her sufferings, forced herself to continue the story, thinking that she could thus satisfy the child's expectant curiosity. But she, sobbing and with her face bathed in tears, said "Mamma, the chair!" trying in this way to tell her mother that she should have stayed in the chair.

She was no longer interested in the story. Both mother and pillows had changed positions. The story had begun in one room and had been continued in another. This had created a dramatic conflict in the mind of the little girl.

These examples indicate the intensity of this instinct. What is perhaps surprising is its extreme precocity. In a child of two years the need for order manifests itself in a tranquil fashion. It is at this time that the need becomes a principle of activity and provides one of the most interesting phenomena to be observed in our schools. When an object is out of place it is a child who perceives it and sets about putting it where it belongs. A child of this age notices a lack of order in the least details which escape the notice of adults and even older children. If, for example, a piece of soap is lying on a washstand and not in the soap-dish, if a chair is out of place, it is a child of two who suddenly notices it and puts it in order.

The sight of something out of place seems to represent a kind of stimulus, a call to activity. But without doubt it is also something more. Order is one of the needs of life which, when it is satisfied, produces a real happiness. In fact, in our schools, even older children, those three- or four-years old, after finishing an exercise will put the things they have used back in place. It is one of the most pleasant and spontaneous tasks they perform. Order consists in recognizing the place for each object in relation to its environment and in remembering where each thing should be. This implies that one is able to orient one's self within one's environment and to dominate it in all its details. The proper environment of the soul is one in which an individual can move about with eyes closed and find, simply by reaching out his hand, anything he desires. Such an environment is necessary for peace and happiness.

Obviously the *love of order* in children is not the same as that of adults. Order provides an adult with a certain amount of external pleasure. But for the small children it is something quite different. It is like the land upon which animals walk or the water in which fish swim. In their first year they derive their principles of orientation from their environment which they must later master. And since a child is formed by his environment he has need of precise and determined guides and not simply some vague constructive formulae.

That order produces a natural pleasure may be seen from the type of games played by very small children. They surprise us with their want of logic. The sole pleasure they afford is that of finding objects in their places. Before illustrating this further I should mention an experiment made by Professor Piaget of Geneva with his own child. He hid an object under the cushion of a chair and then, sending his child out of the room, he took the object and placed it under the cushion of another chair opposite the first. The professor hoped that the child would look for the object under the first cushion and then, when he did not find it, would look for it under another. But all the child did when it returned to the room was to lift up the cushion of the first chair and then say in his own imperfect way, "It's gone." But he made no effort to look for the object elsewhere. Professor Piaget then repeated the experiment, showing the child how he took the object from under one cushion and placed it under another. But the little boy did exactly the same as before and said again, "It's gone." The professor was on the point of concluding that his son was rather stupid. Almost impatiently he lifted the cushion from the second chair and said, "Didn't you see that I put it here?" "Yes," replied the child, and then pointing at the first chair he said, "but it should be there."

The child was not interested in finding the object, but in finding it in its place. He obviously thought that it was the professor who did not understand the game. What object was there to the game if it was not that of putting something in its proper place?

I once witnessed a game of hide and seek played by children who were two or three years old and I was really amazed. They seemed happy, excited, and full of expectation in what they were doing. But this is how they played their game. A child would bend down and crawl under a table covered with a cloth that reached to the floor. The children after seeing him do this would go out of the room and then return, lift the cloth and give a shout of joy as they found their companion behind it. The game was repeated over and over again. They took turns at saying, "Now, I am hiding myself," and then go under the table. On another occasion I saw larger children playing a game of hide and seek with a small child. He hid himself behind a piece of furniture and the older children came in and pretended not to see him. They looked everywhere except behind the furniture, thinking that in this way they would please the tot. But he suddenly cried out, "Here I am," in a tone that obviously implied, "Didn't you see that I was here?"

One day I took part in such a game. I found a group of small children who were shouting and clapping their hands in glee because they had found their companion hidden behind a door. They came up to me and said, "Play with us, hide yourself." I accepted the invitation, and they all ran faithfully out of the room as if they did not want to see where I would hide. Instead of going behind the door, I hid in a corner behind a cabinet. The children returned and went to look for me behind the door in a group. I waited for a while and, finally, seeing that they did not look for me, I came out of my hiding. The children were sad and confused and asked, "Why didn't you play with us? Why didn't you hide yourself?"

If the object of games is pleasure (and as a matter of fact the children were happy in repeating their absurd exercise), it must be confessed that at a certain period a child's life pleasure consists in finding things in their proper places. "Hiding" is interpreted by them as putting or finding something in a concealed spot as if they said to themselves, "You cannot see it, but I know where it is and can find it with my eyes closed."

All this shows that nature endows a child with a sensitiveness to order. It is a kind of inner sense that distinguishes the relationships between various objects rather than the objects themselves. It thus makes a whole of an environment in which the several parts are mutually dependent. When a person is oriented in such an environment, he can direct his activity to the attainment of specific goals. Such an environment provides the foundation for an integrated life. What good is there in an accumulation of various images if they are not arranged according to some order? This would be like having furniture without a house in which to put it. One who knows various objects but does not understand their mutual relations is like one living in a state of chaos from which he cannot extricate himself. It is in childhood that man learns to guide and direct himself on the way of life. The first incentive is given by nature in the sensitive period that is connected with order. Nature, as it were, gives man a compass that will enable him to orientate himself in the world. She is like a teacher who gives her class its first notions of geography by furnishing them with a plan of the classroom. Nature gives children the power to reproduce the sounds of adult speech. Man's intelligence does not come from nothing; rather, it is built upon the foundations laid by a child during his sensitive periods.

THE INNER ORDER

A child has a twofold sense of order. One of these is external and pertains to his perception of his relations with his environment. The second is internal and makes him aware of the different parts of his own body and their relative positions. This type of sensitiveness could be called "inner orientation."

Inner orientation has been studied by experimental psychologists. They have recognized the existence of a muscular sense which enables an individual to become aware of the different positions taken by the various parts of his body and which requires a special kind of memory, the "muscular memory."

Such an explanation is completely mechanistic, based as it is on the experience of consciously performed actions. It is claimed, for example, that if an individual moves his hand to grasp something, the motion is perceived and becomes fixed in the memory and can thus be reproduced. A man can thus choose to move his right or left arm, to turn in one direction or another because of the rational and voluntary experiences which he has previously had.

But a child shows that he passes through a highly developed sensitive period with respect to the various positions of his body long before he can freely move about and have these experiences. In other words, nature furnishes the child with a special sensibility connected with the various attitudes and positions of his body.

The older theories were based on the mechanism of the nervous system. The sensitive periods, on the other hand, are connected with psychic facts. They are insights and impulses that lay the foundation for consciousness. They are spontaneous energies giving rise to fundamental principles that form the basis of psychic growth. Nature, therefore, provides the potentiality and conscious experience for the actual development. A negative proof of the existence and acuteness of this sensitive period may be seen when circumstances arise in the environment which hinder the tranquil development of this creative conquest. When this happens, a child becomes violently agitated and the tantrum, which can resist all attempts to cure it as long as the harmful circumstances persist, can assume the appearance of a disease.

As soon as the obstacle is removed, however, both

tantrum and sickness disappear, showing the obvious cause of the phenomenon.

An interesting example of this may be seen in the experience of an English nurse who had to leave her charge for a short time. She found a capable substitute, but the latter experienced great difficulty in bathing the child entrusted to her care. Whenever he was bathed, he became agitated and desperate. Tears were not his only reaction. He recoiled from the nurse and attempted to push her away in his efforts to escape. The nurse did everything she could think of for the child, but he gradually came to dislike her. When the first nurse returned, the child recovered his composure and was obviously delighted with his bath. The nurse, who had been trained in one of our schools and was interested in discovering the psychological basis for the child's aversion, set about patiently interpreting the child's imperfect speech.

She was able to discover two things: The infant had taken the second nurse to be bad, but why? Because she had given him his bath in reverse. The two nurses then compared the way in which they bathed the child and discovered this difference: the first took the child with her right hand near his head and her left near his feet; the second nurse did just the opposite.

Another case I can recall was more serious in that it had all the appearances of an undetermined malady. I happened to get involved in it and, although I did not directly intervene in my capacity as a physician, I was still able to be of assistance. The child concerned was less than a year-and-a-half old. His mother and father had completed a very long trip and it was their opinion that the child had simply been too small to endure the fatigue. They noted, however, that there had been no particular incidents on the way. Every night they had slept in first-class hotels where a crib had been made ready and special food prepared for the infant. The family was now living in a spacious furnished apartment. Since there was no crib in it, the child was sleeping in a large bed with his mother. The first symptoms of his illness were sleeplessness and an upset stomach. The child had to be carried about at night. His cries were attributed to stomach ache. Pediatricians were called in to examine the child. He was given a special diet, sunbaths, promenades, and other remedies. But these proved to be of no avail, and the nights became an agony for the whole family. The child finally went into convulsions and could be seen writhing on his bed in pitiable spasms. These attacks occurred as often as two or three times a day. An appointment was then made with a famous specialist in nervous diseases of children. It was here that I intervened. The child seemed to be well and, according to his parents, he had been in good health during the course of their long trip. It seemed likely that there was some psychic basis for his disorders. I got this impression as I saw the child lying on a spread suffering one of his attacks. I took two pillows and laid them parallel to each other so that they formed a kind of small bed with vertical sides like a crib. I then covered this with sheets and a blanket and, without saying anything, put the improvised crib next to the child's bed. The little fellow looked at it, ceased to scream, rolled over and over until he came to the edge of the bed, and then dropped himself into the crib saying: "Cama, cama, cama!" the word he used for cradle, and immediately fell asleep. His trouble never returned.

Obviously the child in the large bed had missed the support which his little body had found in the sides of a crib. This lack created a disorder and painful interior conflict that seemed incurable. His reaction illustrates the strength of the sensitive periods, when nature is in the process of creating.

A child does not have the same feeling for order that we do. Experience has made us indifferent. But a child is poor and in the process of gaining impressions. He starts from nothing and feels the fatigue of creation. We are like the sons of a man who has become wealthy through the sweat of his brow. We fail to comprehend the toil and labors he endured. We are cold and thoughtless because of our established position in society. We can now use the reason which the child begot in us, the will which he trained, the muscles which he animated for us. If we can orientate ourselves in the world, it is because the child has given us the means of doing so. And if we are conscious of ourselves, it is because the child has made this possible. We are rich because we are the heirs of the child who started with nothing and provided us with the foundation of our future life. In passing from nothing to that which will be the first principles of one's future life, a child must make tremendous efforts. He is so near to the very founts of life that he acts for the sake of acting. This is the way of creation, of which we have neither knowledge nor remembrance.

9. INTELLIGENCE

A child shows us that intelligence is not built up slowly and from the outside, as is maintained by mechanistic psychologists, who still have great influence in both the theory and practice of education. According to their theory of knowledge, the impressions which we receive from external objects knock upon and, as it were, force the gates of our senses. They then settle down in the psychic area and by gradually associating with each other become organized and build up the mind.

The ancient saying, "There is nothing in the intellect which was not first in some way in the senses," could be applied to this process. It presumes that a child is psychologically passive and at the mercy of his surroundings. From this it would follow that he is absolutely subject to the control of adults. A similar concept is that a child is not only passive mentally but that he is like an empty vase, that is, an object to be filled and molded.

Our experiences certainly do not lead us de-emphasize the importance of a child's environment for the development of his mind. As is well known, our educational system esteems a child's environment so highly that it makes it the center of instruction. We also have a higher and more rational esteem for a child's sensations than other systems of education, but there is a subtle difference between our concept and the older view of the child as a merely passive being. We insist upon the child's inner sensibility. A child has a sensitive period which lasts until he is almost five years old and which enables him to assimilate images from his environment in a truly prodigious fashion. He is an observer actively receiving these images through his senses, but this does not mean that he receives them like a mirror. A true observer acts from an inner impulse, a kind of feeling or special taste, and consequently he is selective in his choice of images. This concept was illustrated by James when he said that no one ever sees an object in the totality of its particulars. Each individual sees only a portion of it, that is, he views it in the light of his own sentiments and interests. Thus the same object is described in different ways by different individuals. James's own examples for this phenomenon were brilliant. He noted that, "if you are greatly pleased with a new suit, you will start to notice the clothes of others and thus run the risk of ending up under an automobile."

We may ask what are the special interests of small children which make them pick out particular images in the countless number that they encounter. It is quite obvious that there can be no external impulse that would set off a trend of thought as in the example cited by James above. A child starts from nothing and advances alone. It is the child's reason about which the sensitive periods revolve. The reasoning process, which is natural and creative, grows gradually like a living thing and gains strength at the expense of the images it receives from its surroundings.

The reason provides the initial force and energy. The various images are ordered to serve the reason, and a child absorbs his first images to assist the reason. A child, we might even say, is eager and even insatiable for such images. As we well know, a child is strongly attracted to light, colors, and sounds, and takes a keen delight in them. But we wish to point up the inner phenomenon, that is, the reasoning process insofar as it is a spontaneous movement, even though here it is just beginning. It should be obvious that a child's psychic state deserves our respect and assistance. A child starts with nothing and develops his reason, the specific characteristic of man. And he starts along this path even before he can walk upon his own small feet.

This can perhaps be better clarified by an example than by an explanation. I can recall a particularly moving case of a four-weeks-old infant that had never been out of the house in which he had been born. One day a nurse was holding the child in her arms when his father and his uncle, who happened to live in this same house, were seen together by the child. The two men were of nearly the same height and age. The infant gave a start of surprise and fright at seeing the two men. They were acquainted with our work and set about allaying the child's fears. Still keeping within view of the infant, they separated, one going to the right and the other to the left. The child turned to look at one, and after gazing at him for a while intently, broke into a smile.

But then he suddenly became worried. He turned his head quickly to look at the other. Only after some time did he smile at him. He repeated these actions turning his head from side to side a dozen times and showing alternate signs of concern and relief before he came to realize that there actually were two individuals. These were the only men that the child had ever seen. They had both played with him on different occasions, taking him into their arms and speaking affectionately to him. The child had come to realize that there was a being different from his mother, nurse, and the other women of the household, but he had never seen two men together and had obviously concluded that there was only one man. When he was suddenly confronted with two, he became alarmed.

From the chaos that surrounded him, he had isolated a single man and then, when he was confronted with another, he discovered his first error. At the early age of four weeks he had perceived the fallibility of human reason as he was struggling in the process of incarnation.

If the two men had been unaware of the existence of a child's psychic life from the moment of his birth, they would not have been able to assist him in the process of obtaining greater awareness.

Examples from the experiences of older children could also be cited. A child of six months was sitting on the floor playing with a pillow. The cover of the pillow was decoracted with pictures of flowers and children, and the child was smelling the flowers and kissing the children with obvious delight. A maid entrusted with his care, but poorly instructed, thought that the child would be pleased if he could smell and kiss other objects as well. So she hastened to bring him various things saying, "Smell this! Kiss this!" But the result was that the child's mind, which was in the process of organizing itself by recognizing pictures and fixing them in his memory and thus happily and peacefully carrying out the work of inner construction, was confused. His mysterious efforts to obtain an inner harmony had been disrupted by an adult who failed to realize what was happening.

Adults can hinder this inner toil when they rudely interrupt a child's reflection or try to distract him. They take the tiny hand of a child, or kiss him, or try to make him go to sleep without taking into account his peculiar psychic development. Through their ignorance adults can thus suppress a child's primitive desires.

It is absolutely necessary, on the other hand, that a child preserve the images which he receives in all their clearness, since it is only through the clarity of these impressions and the distinctions that he makes among them that he can mold its own intellect.

An interesting experiment has been made by a specialist in the feeding of infants. He had founded a clinic and his experience had led him to conclude that individual factors have to be taken into account in the feeding of children. He found that there was no single substitute for a mother's milk that could be given to all children, at least until they had reached a certain age, since what was good for one child could be bad for another. His clinic was a model both physically and esthetically. His procedures produced excellent results in children to the age of six months, but after that they began to lose ground. This was a real puzzle since it is much easier to feed children artifically at this age than earlier. Within the clinic the professor had opened up a dispensary for poor mothers unable to nurse their children who came to him for advice on how to feed them. But these children of poor parents showed no disturbing symptoms after the sixth month as happened with those who were kept in the clinic. After repeated observations the professor came to the conclusion that there must be psychic elements behind this phenomenon, and he began to see that children over six months old in his clinic were suffering from "ennui due to lack of psychic nourishment." When he provided the children with amusements and distractions by having them taken on walks no longer on the terraces of the clinic alone but to places that were new to the infants, they regained their health.

Numerous experiments have conclusively shown that children in their first year receive such clear sensible impressions of their surroundings that they can recognize them in pictures. But it may be further noted that such impressions once gained soon lose their lively interest.

From the beginning of its second year a child is no longer carried away by gaudy objects and brilliant colors with that transport of joy so characteristic of the sensitive periods, but becomes interested in tiny objects that escape our notice. We might even say that he is interested in what is invisible, or at least in what is found on the fringes of consciousness.

I noticed this sensibility for the first time in a little girl fifteen months old. I heard bursts of laughter coming from her in the garden, quite unusual for such a small child. She had gone off by herself and was sitting on the bricks of the terrace. Nearby was a magnificent bed of geraniums blooming under an almost tropical sun. But the child was not looking at them. She had her eyes fixed on the ground, where there was apparently nothing to be seen. I was confronted by one of those childish whims that can be so puzzling. I went up to her slowly and looked carefully at the bricks without being able to see anything in particular. Then the child explained to me in almost measured tones, "A small thing is moving there." Helped by this remark I saw a microscopic, almost inperceptible insect of practically the same color as the bricks running with great rapidity. What had struck the child's fancy was the fact that there was such a small being and that it moved and even ran! Her wonderment broke out in a joyous shout, a shout even louder than usual in such a little child, and the joy was not from the sun, nor the flowers, nor the brilliant colors about her.

A little boy of nearly the same age once impressed me in a similar way. His mother had put together a large collection of colored postcards for him to play with. The child seemed interested and brought me the collection. In his childish speech he said to me, "bam-bam," that is, "automobile." And I realized that he wanted to show me the picture of an automobile.

He had a great many different beautiful pictures and it was obvious that his mother had collected them in order to please and instruct her child at the same time.

On the cards there were pictures of strange animals such as bears, lions, giraffes, and monkeys. There were others also with pictures of birds and domestic animals that should have interested the child—sheep, cats, donkeys, horses, and cows. And there were still others portraying various scenes and landscapes with houses, animals, and human beings. What seemed rather strange, however, was that there was no picture of an automobile in the collection. "I don't see any automobile," I told the child. Then he looked at me, picked out a postcard and said triumphantly, "Here it is!" In the center of the picture could be seen a beautiful hunting dog, in the distance was a hunter with a gun on his shoulder, in one corner could be seen a cottage and winding line that must have been intended as a road, and on the line could be seen a dark spot. The child pointed to it with his finger and said, "bam-bam," and, as a matter of fact, though it was so small as to be almost invisible, I could see that the dot actually did represent an automobile. The fact that a car could be portrayed in such minute proportions and the difficulty of seeing it had attracted the child's interest and prompted him to show it to me.

I thought perhaps that the child's attention had not been drawn to the many beautiful and useful objects portrayed on the cards. I picked out one with the picture of a giraffe on it and began to explain, "Look at the long neck." "Graff," the child answered seriously. I lacked the courage to continue.

It could be said that there is a period in a child's second year when nature leads the intelligence through progressive stages until he gains a knowledge of everything.

The following are some examples of this. I once wanted to show a little boy about twenty months old a beautiful book intended for adults. It was a copy of the New Testament illustrated by Gustave Doré. Among the famous pictures which were reproduced in it was the *Transfiguration* by Raphael. I showed the little fellow a picture of Christ calling children to himself and I began to explain:

"Here is a child right in the arms of Jesus. Others, as you see, are resting their heads against him. All are looking up at him and loving him."

The child's face did not show the least interest. Then, acting as if I did not care, I turned the pages and began to look for another picture. Suddenly the child said, "He is sleeping."

Puzzled by this childish riddle, I asked, "Who is sleeping?"

"Jesus," the child replied earnestly. "Jesus is sleeping." And he made a sign for me to turn back the pages so that I could see it for myself.

I looked at the picture again and saw that it represented Christ looking down upon the children. His eyelids, as a consequence, were lowered like one who was sleeping. The child's attention had been attracted by a detail that no adult would have noticed.

I continued my explanation of the pictures and paused at the one representing Christ's transfiguration. "Look," I said, "Jesus is raised above the earth and the people are frightened. See how the boy twists his eyes, and how the woman is stretching out her arms?" I realized that I had not chosen a suitable picture and that the explanation was not likely to appeal to a child, but I was interested in finding out the difference between the response of a small child and that of an adult to such a complex picture. He simply gave a little grunt as if he were saying, "All right, but keep turning the pages." His small face showed no sign of interest. I began to turn the pages again and saw him grasp a trinket hanging from his neck in the shape of a rabbit. Then he said, "Bunny!" "He has been distracted by the trinket," I thought, but suddenly the child again motioned for me to turn back the pages. I did so and noticed that there actually was a small rabbit represented on one side of the picture of the *Transfiguration*. Who would ever have observed it? Obviously children and adults are in possession of two different mental outlooks, and it is not simply a question of degree, of passing gradually from what is less to what is more.

Adults frequently attempt to point out ordinary objects to three- or four-year-old children as if they had never seen anything before. But this must have the same effect on a child as one shouting at another whom he thinks to be deaf. After making great efforts to be heard, he hears the protest, "But I am not in the least deaf!"

Adults have taken it for granted that children are sensible only to gaudy objects, bright colors, and shrill sounds, and they make use of these to attract a child's attention. We have all noticed how children are attracted by songs, by the tolling of bells, by flags fluttering in the wind, by brilliant lights, and so forth. But these violent attractions are external and transitory, and can be more of a distraction than boon. We might make the comparison with our own way of acting. If we are busy reading an interesting book and suddenly hear a loud band passing by in the street, we get up and go to the window to see what is happening. If we were to see someone act in this way, we would hardly conclude that men are particularly attracted by loud sounds. And yet we make this conclusion about little children. The fact that a strong, external stimulus catches a child's attention is merely incidental and has no real relation with the inner life of the child which is responsible for his development. We can perceive evidence of a child's inner life in the way he immerses himself in the fixed contemplation of minute things that are of no concern to us. But one who is attracted by the smallness of an object and focuses his attention upon it does so, not because it has made a striking impression upon him, but simply because his contemplation of it is an expression of an affectionate understanding.

For adults a child's mind is an unfathomable riddle. It is puzzling to them because they judge it by its outward manifestations rather than by its inner psychic energies. We should try to understand that there is an intelligible reason behind a child's activities. He does nothing without some reason, some motive. It is easy to say that every childish reaction is a whim, but a whim is something more. It is a problem to be solved, a riddle to be answered. It may at times be difficult to find the answer, but the search can be extremely interesting. And if an adult would find the answer to these riddles, he must adopt a new attitude toward the child and deepen his sense of responsibility toward him. He must become a student rather than a thoughtless ruler or tyrannical judge, as he only too often is with respect to a child.

Here I can recall a discussion of a group of women on books for children. "There are some books," a young mother was saying, who had her young son of about eighteen months with her, "that are quite silly and are illustrated with grotesque pictures. I have one of these, *Little Black Sambo*. Sambo is a little Negro who receives various gifts from his parents on his birthday, a cap, shoes, stockings, and a bright colored frock. While his parents are preparing a fine dinner for him, Sambo, anxious to show off his new clothes, leaves the house unnoticed. On the street he meets many wild animals and, in order to pacify them, he has to give something to each one. He gives his cap to a giraffe, his shoes to a tiger, and so on. Eventually he returns home naked and in tears, but the story ends happily for his parents forgive him and set before him a fine dinner, as may be seen on the last page of the book."

The woman passed the book around for the others to see. But the child suddenly said, "No, Lola." Everybody was surprised. What was the little fellow trying to say as he kept repeating, "No, Lola"?

"Lola" his mother said, "is the name of the nurse who has had charge of him for some days." But then her little boy began to cry, "Lola" louder than ever, as if he had fallen into a senseless whim. Finally, we showed him the book and he pointed to the last picture. It was not within the text of the story but inside the cover and represented the poor little Negro crying. We then understood what he meant by, "Lola." It was his way of pronouncing the Spanish, "llora," meaning, "He is crying."

And the child was right. The last picture in the book did not represent a happy scene but Sambo in tears. No one had paid any attention to it. The child's protests were thus perfectly logical when he heard his mother say, "It all ends happily."

The boy had obviously looked more closely than his mother at the book and had seen that the last picture was one of Sambo in tears. His exact observation even though he had not been able to follow the women's conversation in its entirety was certainly striking.

A child's psychic personality is far different from our own, and it is different in kind and not simply in degree.

A child who gathers in the smallest details must look upon us with a certain degree of contempt since he is unaware of the mental syntheses which we are constantly making. He must as a consequence look upon us as being somewhat inefficient, as individuals who do not see well. From a child's viewpoint we are not very exact. He sees us as dull and indifferent since we are not interested in minute details. If a child could express himself, he would certainly tell us that deep down he has little confidence in us, just as we have little confidence in him, since our separate ways of thinking are so foreign to each other.

This is why a child and an adult fail to understand each other.

10. OBSTACLES TO GROWTH

SLEEP

The conflict between child and adult begins when the child reaches a stage in his development when he can act independently. No one can, of course, completely prevent a child from seeing and hearing, and thus making a sensible conquest of his world. But when a child begins to act on his own, to walk, to touch various objects, it is quite a different story. Even though an adult may truly love a child, there rises up within him a powerful defensive instinct. The two psychic states, that of the growing child and that of the adult, are so much at odds that it becomes practically impossible for the two to live together without making some adjustments. And there should be no difficulty in seeing that these adjustments are made to the disadvantage of the child, whose social status is one of absolute inferiority. A child's acts which are not in harmony with an adult environment will inevitably be checked, especially since the adult is not aware of his own defensive attitude but is rather convinced of his generous love and dedication.

But this unconscious defense on the part of the adult flourishes only under a mask. An adult's avarice, which makes him jealously defend whatever he owns, is concealed under "the duty of properly educating one's child." And the fear of having one's peace disrupted is concealed under "the need of making a child sleep a great deal to safeguard his health."

An uneducated woman might defend herself from her child with shouts, slaps, abuse, and by driving it out of the house into the street. But she alternates such acts with loving caresses and ardent kisses that reflect the tender love which she actually has for the child.

The formalism inherent in the higher ranks of society only accepts certain attitudes, such as love, sacrifice, a sense of responsibility, and outward self-control. Nevertheless, women of these higher classes are even more ready to rid themselves of their children's importunities than others of the lower classes. They consign their children to a nurse who will take them for a walk or put them to sleep.

The patience, kindness, and even submissiveness of these women towards the nurses they employ are an indication of a real, if tacit, understanding that they will put up with anything so long as a troublesome child is kept at a reasonable distance.

Hardly has a child learned to move about and begun to exult in his own freedom of activity than he is met by a swarm of giants that block his every move. The child is in a position not unlike that of the Hebrews whom Moses led out of Egypt. After they had overcome the hardships of the desert and were on the point of entering an oasis they were faced with war. The bitter remembrance of the hostile resistance of the Amalekites filled them with such dread that they wandered aimlessly in the desert for forty years, where many perished from exhaustion.

It is almost a law of nature for men to defend their possessions from invaders. Among nations this tendency can become extremely violent. The source of this instinctive self-defense lies hidden in the subconscious depths of the human soul. The earliest and least perceptible manifestation of this cruel phenomenon is found in the care which adults take to preserve their own peace and property against the onslaughts of the new generation, but despite their efforts, the invaders are not checked. They fight desperately, for they are fighting for their lives.

This struggle between the love of the parents and the innocence of the child is carried on unconsciously.

It is quite easy for an adult to say, "A child should not

move about. He should not touch things that do not belong to him. He should not speak out or shout. He should lie down a great deal. He should eat and sleep. He should go out of the house," even if this is to be in the company of a person who is not a member of the family and who has no particular love for the child. Through sheer inertia parents choose the easiest road for themselves. They put their children to sleep.

Who would hesitate to say that a child must sleep?

But if a child is so alert and so quick to observe, he is not a "sleeper" by his very nature. He has need of, and certainly should get, a normal amount of sleep, but it is necessary to distinguish between what is suitable and what is artifically induced. A stronger person through suggestion can impose his own will upon one who is weaker. An adult who forces a child to sleep more than he needs is unconsciously forcing his own will upon the child through the power of suggestion.

Adults, whether they be learned or unlearned parents, or nurses charged with the care of infants, have conspired to condemn this living, active being to sleep. In the homes of the wealthy, infants and even children two, three, or four years old, are condemned to sleep more than they should, though this is not the case in families of the poor. Children of such families run about the streets the whole day long and are not put to sleep because they are not a source of weariness to their mothers. As a rule children of these poor families are less nervous than those who come from wealthier homes. One reason for this may be that prolonged sleep has been advocated for the latter. I remember a seven-year-old child confiding to me that he had never seen the stars, since his parents had always put him to sleep before nightfall. "I would like," he told me, "to go to the top of a mountain some night and stretch myself out on the ground so that I could see the stars."

Many parents boast that their children are so used to going to sleep early in the evening that they themselves are always free to go out.

Even a child's bed can be a source of pain. In contrast

to the soft and beautiful crib for an infant and the spacious bed of an adult, a child's bed is a kind of cage raised on high so that his parents or nurses can tend him without the trouble of stooping and where they can leave him without fear that he will fall out and hurt himself. Further, a child's room is darkened so that the light of the new day will not awaken him.

One of the greatest helps that could be given to the psychological development of a child would be to give him a bed suited to his needs and cease making him sleep longer than necessary. A child should be permitted to go to sleep when he is tired, to wake up when he is rested, and to rise when he wishes. This is why we suggest that the typical child's bed should be done away with, as has already been done in many families. The child instead should be given a low couch resting practically upon the floor, where he can lie down and get up as he wishes.

Like all the new helps for a child's psychic life, a low bed is economical. A child has need of simple things, and complicated objects are frequently more of a hindrance than a help to his development. In many families this reform in a child's sleeping habits has been achieved by placing a small mattress on the floor and covering it with a large blanket. A child can thus of his own accord go off cheerfully to bed in the evening and rise in the morning without disturbing anyone. Such examples as these show how wrong adults have been in imposing their own wills upon children and in exhausting themselves in caring for their children. Actually, they were going against their children's needs because of the promptings of their defensive instincts, which could easily have been overcome.

From all this we can see that an adult should strive to interpret the needs of a child so that he can satisfy them by providing him with a suitable environment. Only thus can a new educational epoch be inaugurated that will bring real assistance to humanity. Adults must cease to look upon a child as an object to be lifted and carried about when he is small and which has nothing more to do than obey adults when he is larger. Adults must become convinced that they have a secondary role to play in a child's development. They must endeavor to understand children so that they can properly assist them. This should be the aim and desire of a child's mother as well as of all those who have anything to do with his education. A child is naturally much weaker than an adult. If he is to develop his personality, it is necessary that the adult should hold himself in check and follow the lead given by the child. And he should regard it as a privilege that he is able to understand and follow him.

11. WALKING

The line of conduct to be followed by an adult is that of renouncing his own advantages so that he can accommodate himself to the needs of a growing child.

Higher animals instinctively act in this way when they adapt themselves to the needs of their young. When a baby elephant is brought by its mother into the adult herd, the huge beasts slow their pace to that of the little calf, and when it becomes tired and stops, they all stop as well.

A similar consideration for children is found in various cultures. One day I saw a Japanese father taking his little son for a walk. I followed them and noticed that all of a sudden the child, who was about a year-and-a-half or two-years old, put his arms around his father's leg. The man stood still and let the boy spin around his leg, and when he had finished his game, the two started out again at a slow walk. After a little while the child sat down on a curb, while his father stood beside him. The latter's face was grave, but perfectly natural. He was doing nothing exceptional. He was simply a father taking his little son for a walk.

This is the kind of walk best suited for children who are learning how to coordinate the many different movements needed to maintain their balance and advance on two feet.

Although a man has limbs like those of other animals, he must walk on two feet instead of four. Monkeys have very long arms that are of assistance to them when they walk upon the ground. Man is the only animal which actually relies entirely upon his two legs for balanced walking. When quadrupeds walk they alternately lift one front, and one diagonally opposed rear foot as they keep the other two upon the ground. But when a man walks he first supports himself upon one foot and then upon the other. Nature has solved the difficulty of locomotion, but in different ways. Animals learn to walk through instinct, but man learns to walk through personal, voluntary effort.

A child develops the ability to walk not by merely waiting for it to come but by walking. His first step, which is greeted with such joy by his parents, is a conquest of nature and marks as a rule the passage from the first to the second year. Learning to walk is for a child a kind of second birth, when he passes from a helpless to an active being. Success in his efforts is one of the primary indications of a child's normal development, but after his first steps, he still has need of constant practice. The attainment of balance and a steady gait is a product of continuous individual effort. A child is driven on by an irresistible impulse in his attempts to walk. He is courageous and even rash in his attempts and, like a true soldier, he drives on toward victory regardless of the risks encountered. The very eagerness with which a child pursues this goal prompts adults to surround him with safeguards that are actually obstacles. They try to keep a child shut up within a playpen or strapped into a stroller in which he will take his exercise even after his legs are strong.

When the child is taken out, he is pushed around in a buggy even though he could walk; but since his legs are short and he does not have the endurance for long walks, he must accommodate himself to the adult who refuses to give up his own pace. Even when the adult who is taking the child out is a nurse, it is the child who has to adapt himself to the nurse and not the nurse to the child. A nurse will go at her own speed directly for the predetermined goal of the outing, pushing the baby carriage with the child in it as she would a cart loaded with vegetables. It is only when she reaches the park that she will take the child out of the carriage, sit down, and allow the child to walk about on the grass as she keeps a watchful eye on him. All this is done simply to shield a child from possible accidents. Care is taken of his physical growth but not of his inner psychic development.

A child between the ages of a year and a half and two can walk several miles and clamber up such difficult objects as ramps and stairs, but he has an entirely different purpose in walking than we do. An adult walks to reach some external goal and he consequently heads straight for it. He has a steady gait, which carries him along almost mechanically. An infant, on the other hand, walks to perfect his own proper functions, and consequently his goal is something creative within himself. He is slow, he does not as yet have a rhythmical pace nor does he direct his steps toward some ultimate external goal. He moves on attracted by the objects he sees immediately about him. If an adult is to assist such a child, he must give up his own pace and his own finality.

I once knew at Naples a couple whose youngest child was a year and a half old. To reach the sea during the summer, they had to descend nearly a mile down a steep road that was practically impassable for wagons or carriages. The young parents wanted to have their child with them, but found it too fatiguing to carry him in their arms. The child himself solved the problem by walking and running the whole length of the way. Every now and then he would stop by some flowers, or sit down in the grass, or stand to look at some animals. On one occasion he stood fixed for almost fifteen minutes staring at a donkey grazing in a field. Moving slowly forward in this way the child was able to descend and ascend the long and difficult road each day without becoming weary.

In Spain I came to know two children between the ages of two and three who would take walks a mile and a half in length and many others who spent more than an hour descending and ascending steep stairs with very narrow steps.

Even with respect to activities such as these, there are mothers who speak about the whims of their children. A woman once asked me about the tantrums of her little girl who had been walking for only a few days. Whenever she saw a stairs, she began to shriek, and when anyone would pick her up to carry her up or down the stairs, she would become almost frantic. Her mother thought that she might possibly be mistaken about the cause of the child's outbursts. It seemed unreasonable that the child should become so tearful and agitated whenever she was being carried up or down stairs. And she thought that the disturbance might simply have been coincidental. But it was obvious that the little girl simply wanted to climb up and down the stairs by herself. She was more attracted by the steps, upon which she could rest her hands or sit down, than by the open field where her feet were buried in the tall grass and where she found nothing on which to place her hands. And yet the only place where she had been permitted to wander about was in these fields.

Children naturally like to walk and move around, and open stairs will always be filled with them as they climb up and down and scramble about. The ease with which a child from a poor family darts about the streets avoiding traffic and even catching rides on cars and trucks reveals, despite its hazards, a potentiality far removed from the sluggishness of a timid, and ultimately lazy, child of the upper classes. But neither child has been really assisted in his development. The poor child is abandoned to the dangerous adult environment of the streets. The other is hindered by being hedged in by too many things meant to save him from the dangers inherent in these same surroundings.

A child on his way to becoming a man and thus continuing the human race is like the Messias of whom it was said, he "has nowhere to lay his head."

12. THE HAND

It is interesting to note that two of the three great steps regarded by physiologists as criteria for the normal development of a child are concerned with movement, that is, with learning how to walk and how to speak. These two motor functions are kind of a horoscope in which a child's future may be read. In fact, these complex activities show that a child has gained his first victory over his means of motion and expression. But if language is a specific characteristic of man in as much as it is an expression of his thought, walking is something which he shares with all other animals.

An animal is different from a vegetable in that "it moves about in space." And when such movement is effected through special organs like the limbs, its manner of walking becomes a fundamental characteristic. Nevertheless, even though man's ability to move about in space is so great that it has permitted him to encompass the whole earth, walking of itself is not a specific characteristic of an intelligent being.

Instead, the two bodily movements most intimately connected with man's intelligence are those of the tongue, which he uses for speaking, and those of his hands, which he employs for work. Man's presence in certain localities in prehistoric times is deduced from the chipped and polished stones which he used for his first tools. The ability to use tools marks a new stage in the biological history of living creatures here on earth. Speech itself becomes a record of man's past when it is recorded on rock through the work of his hands. One of man's special characteristics is the freedom with which he can use his hands. His upper limbs become instruments of his intelligence rather than means of locomotion. Because of the use which he makes of his limbs in the service of his intelligence, man not only shows that he occupies a higher state than other creatures but he also indicates the fundamental unity of his human nature.

The human hand, so delicate and so complicated, not only allows the mind to reveal itself but it enables the whole being to enter into special relationships with its environment. We might even say that man "takes possession of his environment with his hands." His hands under the guidance of his intellect transform this environment and thus enable him to fulfill his mission in the world.

It seems logical that if we wish to determine the mental development of a child we should consider his "intelligent movements" from their first appearance, that is, that we should study his speech and the use which he makes of his hands in working.

Men have instinctively recognized the importance of these two external manifestations of the intellect, that is, of speech and human gestures, and have implicitly recognized them as being specific characteristics of the human race. But they have done so only with respect to certain symbols connected with the social life of adults. When a man and a woman, for example, marry, they join hands and "pledge their troth." When a man becomes engaged he "makes a promise," or "gives his word," and the woman is "asked for her hand." In taking an oath, one raises his hand when he pronounces the words. The hands are symbolically employed in rituals where there is a strong expression of the ego. To clear himself of the responsibility of Christ's death Pilate literally and figuratively washed his hands before the crowd. Before beginning the most solemn portion of the Mass, a priest at the altar will say, "I will wash my hands among the innocent," and as he pronounces these words he actually washes his fingers, even though he has done this before approaching the altar.

These various illustrations can show how men subconsciously regard the hand as a manifestation of the inner ego. If this is so, what can be more wonderful and sacred than the development within the child of this essentially "human activity." The first movement of his small hand toward external objects should thus be eagerly awaited.

The first intelligent moving of these tiny hands, the first thrust of that movement which represents the effort of the ego to penetrate the world should fill an adult's mind with admiration. But instead he is *afraid* of those tiny hands stretching out for things that are of no value and importance in themselves, and he strives to keep them from the child. He is constantly saying, "Don't touch!" just as he constantly repeats, "Be still! Keep quiet!"

And in this anxiety that lurks in the shadows of his subconsciousness the adult erects a defense and calls upon the assistance of other men, as if he had to struggle secretly against a power that was attacking his comfort and possessions.

In order to develop his mind a child must have objects in his environment which he can hear and see. Since he must develop himself through his movements, through the work of his hands, he has need of objects with which he can work that provide motivation for his activity. But within the family circle this need has been neglected. The objects which surround a child belong to adults and are destined for their use. As far as the child is concerned they are taboo. A crucial factor in his development is settled by telling him not to touch anything. If a child succeeds in grasping something, he is like a hungry puppy that has found a bone and goes off to a corner to gnaw on it, seeking nourishment from something that cannot provide it and fearful that someone will chase him away.

A child's movements are not due to chance. Under the direction of his ego he builds up the necessary coordination for organized movement. At the expense of countless intervening experiences, his ego coordinates, organizes, and unifies his organs of expression with his developing psyche. The child must therefore be free to determine and execute his own acts. Since he is in the process of molding himself, his movements have a special character that is not simply the result of chance or random impulses. A child does not simply run, jump, and handle things without purpose and thus create havoc about the house. His constructive movements take their cue from the actions of others. He strives to imitate them in the way they use or handle something. A child tries to act like the adults about him, making use of the same objects. His activity therefore will be directly connected with his family and social environment. A child will want to sweep the floor, wash dishes or clothes, pour out water, wash himself, comb his hair, clothe himself, and so forth. This natural tendency of a child has been called "imitation." But the expression is not exact since it differs, for example, from the mimetic actions of monkeys. A child's constructive movements have a psychic origin and are of an intellectual nature. Knowledge always precedes movement. When a child wishes to do something, he knows beforehand what it is. He has seen another do something and he is anxious to do it himself. This is true with his learning how to speak. A child picks up the language that he hears spoken about him. He carries with him the memory of the word that he has previously heard. But he uses the word himself according to the particular needs of the moment.

In his use of words the child is not like a parrot. He does not simply imitate a sound but makes use of knowledge that has been acquired and stored up. A child's imitation is never purely mechanical. We must realize this if we would appreciate more intimately a child's activities and his relations with adults.

ELEMENTARY ACTIONS

Before a child can carry out actions in a clearly logical fashion like the adults whom he observes, he begins to act for his own ends, using objects in a way that is often unintelligible to his elders. This often happens with children who are between a year and a half and three years old. I once saw, for example, a child of eighteen months who had found a pile of recently ironed napkins neatly stacked one upon the other. The little fellow took one of these napkins and held it with the greatest care. He placed one of his hands over it so that it would not become unfolded and carried it diagonally across the room to the opposite corner where he set it on the floor saying, "One." He then returned as he had come, a sure indication that he was being guided by some special sensibility. After he had crossed the room, he took a second napkin in the same way, carried it by the same route, and placed it on the one already on the floor, and again said, "One." He repeated this operation until he had carried all the napkins over to the other corner. Then reversing the process, he carried them all back singly to their original place. Although the pile of napkins was no longer in the perfect condition in which it had originally been left, they were still fairly well folded and the stack, although somewhat askew, was not actually disordered. Fortunately for the child no member of the family was present during this long maneuver. How often do small children hear adults at their backs shouting, "Stop! Stop! Leave that alone!" And how often their tiny, tender hands are slapped to teach them not to touch anything!

Another "elementary" task that fascinates children is to take a stopper out of a bottle and replace it, especially if the stopper is of cut glass reflecting the colors of the rainbow. This task of pulling out and putting back stoppers seems to be one of their favorite occupations. Another favorite activity of a child is to lift up and lower the cover of a large inkstand or box, or even to open and shut the door of a cabinet. It is quite understandable that a conflict should frequently occur between a child and an adult over objects that have a natural attraction for youngsters but which they are forbidden to touch since they belong to mother's or father's desk, or are a part of the living-room furniture. Such a conflict can induce a tantrum. But a child does not really want a particular bottle or inkstand. He would be satisfied with objects of his own that would enable him to go through these same movements.

Such elementary actions as these, which have no external finality, can be regarded as the first feeble efforts of the human worker. Some of the material which we have devised for very small children, such as graduated cylinders that fit snugly into holes in a block, have been highly successful since they were designed to satisfy the needs of this particular period in a child's life.

The ideal of leaving a child on his own is easily grasped, but there are deeply rooted obstacles in an adult's mind that make it difficult to realize. An older person, even if he wishes to grant a child's desires and leave him free to touch and move objects about, finds that he cannot resist the vague impulses within himself that lead to his dominating the child.

A young woman in New York, who was familiar with these ideas, was anxious to put them into practice with her own two-and-a-half-year-old son. One day she saw him bringing a pitcher full of water into the parlor. She noticed the strain he was under and the efforts he was making as he moved slowly across the room repeating to himself, "Be careful! Be careful!" The pitcher was heavy and the child's mother finally felt compelled to assist him. She took the pitcher and carried it to where he was going, but the child was grieved and mortified. His mother realized that she had caused her child to suffer but she justified her action by saying that even though she appreciated the necessity under which her child was laboring, it seemed wrong to let him tire himself and lose so much time in doing something which she could accomplish in a moment.

"I know that I did wrong," the woman told me as she asked my advice. I reflected on the other aspect of this particular problem, the "stinginess with respect to a child" that rises from a desire to protect one's own possessions. I asked her, "Do you have any good china, some cups for example? Let your child carry one of these light objects and see what happens." The woman followed my advice and told me later that her child had carried the cups with care and attention, pausing at each step and finally setting them down safely at their destination. During the operation the child's mother was torn between two sentiments, one of pleasure at her son's work and the other of worry about her cups. But she let her child complete the task which he was so anxious to perform and which was so important for his psychic development.

On another occasion I put a rag in the hands of a little girl fourteen months old so that she could do some dusting. As she sat, she polished many bright little objects and took great pleasure in her work, but her mother had some difficulty in giving her little daughter an object that seemed to be so foreign to the needs of so small a child.

An adult who does not understand the importance of the instinct to work in a child is surprised at its first manifestation. He sees that he must make some great sacrifices. He must renounce something of his own personality and environment, but this is quite incompatible with his ordinary social life. In adult surroundings a child is certainly an extra-social being. But to completely exclude him from such surroundings, as is still done today, is to stunt his growth, just as if he were not allowed to learn how to speak.

The solution to this conflict is to be found in preparing a suitable environment for the child where he may manifest his higher tendencies. When a child utters his first word, there is no need to prepare anything special for him, since his prattling is heard as a sound of joy within the home. But the work of tiny hands which are the first stammerings of a man at work require "incentives to activity" in the form of objects which correspond to his desire to work. At times one sees children carrying out actions which require an effort going beyond what one would think would be physically possible. I have a photograph of a little English girl carrying a great loaf of bread so large that her two arms can hardly bear it, and she has to hold it tightly against her body. She is forced to walk bent backwards without being able to see where she is putting her feet. In the picture there is also a dog that accompanies her and does not let her out of its sight. It is tense and seems as if it were on the point of leaping forward to assist her. In the background are adults watching the child. They have to restrain themselves from rushing up and taking the bread in their own arms.

Sometimes very small children in a proper environment develop a skill and exactness in their work that can only surprise us.

13. RHYTHM

An adult who does not understand that a child needs to use his hands and does not recognize this as the first manifestation of an instinct for work can be an obstacle to the child's development. This is not always due to a defensive attitude on the part of the adult. There can be other causes as well. One of these is the fact that an adult looks to the external finality of his actions and determines the means which he employs according to his own mental outlook. For him there is a kind of natural law, "the law of minimal effort," which induces him to employ the most direct means that will enable him to attain his goal in the least possible time. When he sees a child making great efforts to perform some seemingly fruitless action which he himself could do in an instant and much more perfectly, he is pained and attempts to assist the child.

To an adult a child's enthusiasm for trivial or useless things is something quite grotesque and even incomprehensible. When a child notices that a tablecloth is askew, he remembers how it should be spread and slowly, with all the enthusiasm at his command, he attempts to straighten it. For a child at this stage of his development, this is a triumphant action; but he will only achieve it if adults keep aloof and refrain from hindering his efforts.

If a child wants to comb his hair, an adult instead of being pleased by this noble ambition, feels assailed to the very fibers of his being. He knows that a child cannot comb his hair well or quickly and that he will not succeed in attaining his goal, whereas he, an adult, can do it quickly and better for the child. Then a child, who has been carrying out a delightful and constructive action, sees the adult, an enormous and powerful being with whom it is useless to contend, come near and take the comb and say that he must do the combing. The same thing happens when an adult sees a child is tiring himself in trying to put on his clothes or tie his shoes. Every attempt of the child is interrupted. The adult is irritated not only by the fact that the child tries fruitlessly to complete an action, but by his very rhythm, by his different manner of acting.

Rhythm is not simply an old concept that can be changed at will. It is an intrinsic characteristic of an individual almost like the shape of his body. We take pleasure in associating with others whose rhythmical movements are like our own but are pained when we are forced to adapt ourselves to other rhythms.

If, for example, we must walk with one who is partially paralyzed we feel a kind of anguish, and if we see another who has had a stroke lift a glass to his lips with a slow and trembling hand, we are pained by the sharp contrast between his halting movement and our own freedom of action. We strive to free ourselves from this inner conflict by substituting our own rhythm for his on the assumption that we are assisting him.

An adult acts somewhat similarly with respect to a child. Unconsciously he strives to keep the child from making his naturally slow and deliberate movements and he would remove this annoyance as he would brush away a fly.

On the other hand, an adult can put up with a child's movements when they are carried out in a swift and rapid rhythm. He is ready to endure the disorder and confusion created by a lively child. Here an adult can "arm himself with patience," since he observes something that is quite clear and understandable; but when a child moves slowly, an adult feels compelled to intervene by substituting his own activity for that of the child. But in acting thus an adult, instead of assisting a child in his psychic needs, substitutes himself in all the actions which the child would like to carry out by himself. He prevents the child from acting freely and thus makes himself the greatest obstacle to the child's natural development. The desperate cries of the "capricious" child who does not want to be washed, dressed, or combed reveal the dramatic struggle that engages a child in his efforts to grow up. Who would ever imagine that the needless assistance given to a child is the first of the various *repressions* which he will experience and one which can have serious consequences in later life?

The Japanese, as a part of their cult of the dead, place a number of small stones and similar objects upon the tombs of children. The stones laid on the tomb by a child's parents will enable him to rebuild the toy castles which he makes, but which are being constantly knocked down by tormenting demons. This concept of the tortures experienced by dead children is one of the most striking examples we have of the projection of the subconscious into the afterlife.

14. THE SUBSTITUTION OF THE PERSONALITY

An adult can substitute himself for a child by acting in his place, but also by subtly imposing his own will, substituting it for that of the child. When this happens it is no longer the child that acts but the adult working through the child.

When Charcot in his famous institute of psychiatry showed that through hypnosis a substitution could be made in the personalities of individuals subject to hysteria, he created a great sensation. His experiments seemed to undermine what had been previously regarded as one of the most basic features of human nature, namely, that a man is master of his own actions. But Charcot proved experimentally that such a strong suggestion could be given to a subject that he lost his own personality and took on that of the hypnotist.

These experiments, even though they were limited in number and carried out in a clinic, opened up the way to new studies and discoveries, such as those dealing with split personalities, with the subconscious, and with sublimated psychic states.

The period of childhood when a child starts to become conscious of himself and his senses are in a creative state is particularly subject to suggestion. During this time an adult can insinuate himself into a child and animate his will and mobility with his own.

We have noticed in our schools that if we show a child how to do something with too much enthusiasm or exaggerated movements, the child's capacity to think and judge for himself is repressed. It could be said that an activity is separated from the child's ego which ought to command him and is taken up by another ego that is stronger but which does not belong to the child. This foreign ego has the power to rob the child of his own tender means of activity. An adult does not, as a rule, willingly do this. But he can dominate a child through his hypnotic suggestions without wishing, or even knowing that he is doing so, without even being aware of the existence of such an influence.

A few examples of this that I have personally encountered may be of interest. I once saw a child about two years old put a pair of dirty shoes on a white bedspread. Impulsively and without much thought, I took the shoes and put them in a corner of the room and said, "They're dirty." I then brushed the spread where they had been placed with my hand. After this incident, the little fellow, whenever he saw a pair of shoes, would run up to them and say, "They're dirty." He would then go over to the bed and pass his hand over it as if to clean it, even though the shoes had been nowhere near it.

Here is another example. A young woman one day received a package. She expressed her happiness at the gift, opened it, and found within the box a silk handkerchief, which she gave to her little daughter, and a trumpet, which she put to her lips and blew. The child shouted with glee, "Music!" And for some time after, whenever she touched a piece of cloth, she would beam and say, "Music!"

Prohibitions on the part of adults, when they are not so emphatic as to provoke a reaction in a child, can easily have an inhibiting influence upon a child's activity. Such a restraining influence comes most frequently from educated, self-controlled adults, and especially from refined nurses. One interesting case is that of a little girl about four years old who was alone with her grandmother at the latter's country estate. The little girl obviously wanted to turn the faucet of a fountain in the garden to see the water gush out. But when she was on the point of doing so, she suddenly drew back her hand. Her grandmother encouraged her to turn the faucet, but the child replied, "No, my nurse does not like it." The child's grandmother then tried to persuade her, telling her that she had permission to do so. The child smiled with pleasure and satisfaction at the thought of seeing the water spurt forth. She stretched out her hand, but then drew it back again without opening the faucet. The bidding of the absent nurse was more compelling than the invitation of the child's grandmother at her side.

A somewhat similar case is that of a somewhat older child, a boy of about seven years. When he was seated and saw something at a distance that attracted him, he would get up and start for the object, but he would then return and sit down as if he suffered from a wavering of his will that he could not overcome. Who was the "master" who checked his steps? No one knew, for the memory had vanished even from the child's mind.

LOVE FOR THE ENVIRONMENT

A child's susceptibility to suggestion can be understood as an exaggeration of an inner sensibility which assists with his psychic growth and which may be called "the love of the environment." A child is an eager observer and is particularly attracted by the actions of adults and wants to imitate them. In this regard an adult can have a kind of mission. He can be an inspiration for the child's actions, a kind of open book wherein a child can learn how to direct his own movements. But an adult, if he is to afford the proper guidance, must always be calm and act slowly so that the child who is watching him can clearly see his actions in all their particulars.

If an adult does not do this but yields instead to his own natural tendencies, then, instead of inspiring the child and instructing him, he will impart his own rapid rhythms upon the soul of the child and substitute himself for the child through the power of suggestion.

Even sense objects, if they are attractive, can have a powerful, suggestive influence upon a child, drawing out various activities like a magnet. A film of an interesting psychological experiment recorded by Professor Levine can help to illustrate this. The object of his experiment was to discern the different reactions to the same objects on the part of defective children and of normal children from one of our schools. Both groups of children were of about the same age and from the same general background. A large table was set up covered with many different objects, including some of the material which we have devised for children's use.

In the film a group of children is seen coming into the room. They are interested and attracted by the various objects set before them. They are lively and their smiles indicate their happiness in the midst of so many different things. Each one of the children takes something and sets to work. He then sets it aside and takes up something else and repeats this, going from one activity to another.

After this part of the film has been shown, a second group of children is seen entering the room. They move slowly, stop, and look around. They barely handle the objects but gather around them and seem to stand inactive. And this brings the second half of the picture to a close.

Which of the two groups was made up of defective, and which of normal children? The deficient children were the happy, lively ones who moved about a great deal, passing from one object to another and playing with everything. To people watching the film, they give the impression of being more intelligent, since adults as a rule are accustomed to look upon vivacious, cheerful children who pass from one thing to another as more intelligent.

But actually, normal children move about in a calm and tranquil manner. In the film they can be seen standing still for a long time and paying thoughtful attention to a single object. They prove in a striking way that calm and measured movement accompanied by thoughtful consideration are the marks of a normal child.

Professor Levine's experiment runs counter to generally accepted notions since, in an ordinary environment, intelligent children will act like the deficient children in the film. A normal child as found in our schools is something new. It is slow and reflective but its movements are controlled by its ego and guided by reason. Such a child is stimulated by the objects it sees, but masters these impressions and as a consequence can make full use of them. Self-control and not ceaseless activity is what counts. It is important that a child should master his motor organs and not simply move about in any manner whatever.

The ability to move about under the guidance of reason and not simply in response to sensible stimuli leads to concentration, and this fixation of the mind and activity upon a single object is a phenomenon of inner origin.

The ability to move oneself in a deliberate and thoughtful manner is actually normal to the individual. It is the mark of an inner discipline which manifests itself in orderly, external acts. When this inner discipline is lacking, an individual's activity can escape his personal control and be directed by the will of another or become a prey to external influences like a ship adrift.

The will of another produces disciplined actions only with difficulty since such an external influence does not create the organization necessary for such activity. When this happens, we can say that the individual's personality has been split. When this occurs in a child, he loses his opportunity to develop as nature intended he should. Such a child might be compared to a man who has landed in a desert with a balloon and who suddenly sees his balloon caught up by the wind leaving him alone. He has lost it and sees nothing about him that can take its place. This is a picture of what can happen to a man when, as a child, he has had to contend with adults. His mind is darkened and undeveloped, and his means of expression are disordered and, as it were, a prey to the elements.

15. MOVEMENT

The importance of physical activity or movement in psychic development should be emphasized. It has been a serious error to list movement among the various functions of the body without adequately distinguishing it from those of the vegetative life such as the assimilation of food, breathing, and so forth. Practically, movement is simply considered as an aid to the normal functioning of the body in its breathing, digesting, and circulation of the blood.

Movement, although it is characteristic of animals, does have an influence also upon the vegetative life. We can almost say that it is something that precedes, accompanies, and follows all bodily activities, and yet it would be wrong to consider movement merely from the physical point of view. We can see the benefits to be derived from engaging in sports. Such physical activities are not only conducive to physical health, but they also inspire courage and self-confidence. They can also have a moral influence in raising one's ideals and in arousing a tremendous enthusiasm among spectators. And these various psychic effects are of a much higher level than those of a purely physical order.

A child develops through personal effort and engagement. His growth, therefore, depends upon psychic as well as physical factors. It is of utmost importance that a child be able to recall the impressions he has received and be able to keep them clear and distinct, since the ego builds up its intelligence through the strength of the sense impressions which it has received. It is through this hidden inner labor that a child's reason is developed. And reason in the final analysis is what distinguishes a man from irrational beings. A man is one who can make a reasoned judgment and then, through an act of the will, decide his own course of action.

Adults adopt the attitude that they can wait for a child's reason to develop with time. They do not attempt to assist it, but rather oppose their own reasoning processes to the child's developing reason. This happens particularly when a child's movements disturb them. But, as we have seen, movement is of great importance for a child. It is the functional incarnation of the creative energy which brings man to the perfection of his species. Through movement, he acts upon his external environment and thus carries out his own personal mission in the world. Movement is not only an impression of the ego but it is an indispensable factor in the development of consciousness, since it is the only real means which places the ego in a clearly defined relationship with external reality. Movement, or physical activity, is thus an essential factor in intellectual growth, which depends upon the impressions received from outside. Through movement we come in contact with external reality, and it is through these contacts that we eventually acquire even abstract ideas. Physical activity connects the spirit with the world, but the spirit has need of action in a twofold sense, to acquire concepts and to express itself exteriorly. Movement, or physical activity, can be extremely complicated. A man's muscles are so numerous that it is impossible for him to use them all. It can even be said that a man always has at his disposal a reservoir of unused organs. A ballerina will make use of muscles which will not be employed at all by a skilled surgeon or mechanic, and vice versa. And the use which one makes of his muscles has an influence upon the development of his personality.

Every individual should take sufficient exercise to keep his muscles in a healthy state. When they are thus conditioned it is possible to develop certain muscles for specialized activities. But if the muscles in general are not sufficiently used, one's vital energies are sapped.

If muscles which should normally be functioning are dormant, there is not only a physical, but a psychic depression as well. This is why action can have an influence also upon one's spiritual energies.

A knowledge of the direct connection that exists between physical activity and the will can make us appreciate more fully the importance of physical motion. All the various vegetative functions of the living being, although they are connected to the nervous system, are independent of the will. Each individual organ has it own proper function which it carries out in a constant fashion.

The different cells and tissues carry out their special tasks. They are like specialists who skillfully carry out their own particular work but who are helpless when they attempt to do something outside of it. The essential difference between these cells and tissues and the muscles lies in the fact that even though the cells that make up the muscles have their own special work to do, they do not act by themselves but need to be given orders, and without such orders they do not act. They might be compared with soldiers who wait for the commands of their higher officers.

Among the cells which have no need of external directions are those which secrete milk or saliva, take in oxygen, combat germs, and which, through their cooperative, unceasing labors, maintain the health of the whole being, just as the efforts of individual laborers contribute to the welfare of society. Their adaptation to specific tasks is essential for the functioning of the whole organism.

In contrast to the fixed activity of these involuntary cells and tissues an individual's muscles should be free and quick to respond to every command of the will. Ready obedience is only acquired through prolonged exercise and practice. Only then can the various groups of muscles that must act together to carry out the command function together as they should.

In carrying out the bidding of the will, a person's body may at times have to perform acts of enormous complexity. Since it is through movement that the will realizes itself, we should assist a child in his attempts to put his will into act. A child has a natural desire to master the voluntary use of his organs of movement. If he fails to do so, he cannot externalize the fruit of his intelligence. The will is thus not only an instrument of execution but also of psychic development.

One of the most interesting and unexpected discoveries in our schools was the love and diligence with which children who acted on their own carried out their tasks. A child who is free to act not only seeks to gather sensible impressions from his environment but he also shows a love for exactitude in the carrying out of his actions. His spirit then seems to be suspended between existence and self-realization. A child is a discoverer. He is an amorphous, splendid being in search of his own proper form.

16. THE LACK OF COMPREHENSION

Since adults have no concept of the importance of physical activity for a child, they put a damper on it as a cause of disturbance.

Even scientists and educators have failed to notice the great importance of movement in human development. Nevertheless, if the very word "animal" connotes "animation" or, simply, "activity," and if the difference between plants and animals lies in the fact that the former are rooted to the earth, while the latter can move about, why should we wish to check a child's movements?

Adults thoughtlessly say, "A child is a plant, a flower," which means, "It ought to be quiet," or that a child is "an angel," that is, a being which moves about, it is true, but outside the world inhabited by men.

All this reveals the mysterious blindness of the human soul, which is even greater than that partial blindness which psychoanalysts recognize as existing in man's subconsciousness. The depth of this blindness may be appreciated from the fact that science, though it has probed man's subconscious depths, has not revealed it.

All agree upon the importance of the sense organs for intellectual growth. It is obvious that one who is deaf or blind will encounter extraordinary difficulties in reaching intellectual maturity since hearing and sight are, as it were, the gates of the mind. Deafness and blindness are handicaps that are compatible with otherwise perfect physical health, but it would be absurd to think that a child would attain a higher standard of culture and morality if he were deliberately deprived of his sight and hearing.

Despite all this, it is not easy to gain acceptance for the idea that physical activity is of great importance for man's moral and intellectual development. If a still growing child fails to use his organs of movement, his development is retarded and he will fall farther short of his goal than if he had been deprived of either sight or hearing.

One who is "a prisoner of the flesh" undergoes more dramatic and profound sufferings than one who is blind or deaf and dumb. Although the deaf and blind are deprived of means of coming into contact with their surroundings, through a process of adaptation, the keenness of their other senses can at least partially make up for those that are lacking. Physical activity on the other hand is intimately connected with one's personality, and there is no substitute for it. One who fails in this regard hurts himself. He turns his back on life and hurls himself into an abyss from which there is no exit. He becomes an everlasting exile like Adam and Eve who, after they had been expelled from the earthly Paradise, had to fare forth full of shame and sorrow into the unknown hardships of an unknown world.

When we speak of "muscles" we usually picture them to ourselves as some sort of a machine. Such a concept is opposed to our concept of a spirit which is free from matter and consequently from any sort of mechanism.

To say that movement or physical activity is more important for the development of the mind than the intellectual senses of sight and hearing would strike most people as rather strange. And yet even our eyes and our ears function according to physical and even mechanical laws. The eye has been described as "a camera informed with life," and certainly it is wonderfully constructed. The ear, too, is not unlike a band with its vibrating chords and drum.

But when we speak of the role played by these stupendous instruments in the development of the mind, we do not look upon them as mechanical devices but as means of acquiring knowledge. Through these wonderful, living instruments the ego comes into contact with the world and uses them for fulfilling its own psychic needs. The soul is constantly being nourished with the sight of natural beauties like the rising of the sun, or the delightful vision of a work of art, or with the sound of melodious voices or instruments. And it is the individual person who enjoys and passes judgment upon these various sense impressions.

If there were no ego to take delight in these various sights and sounds, what good would there be in these elaborate organs of sense? Seeing and hearing are of themselves of little importance, but they have a higher purpose. It is through seeing and hearing that one's personality is molded and developed.

The same is brought about through movement, that is, physical activity. This requires various organs, even if these organs are not so highly specialized as the eardrum or the lens of the eye. A fundamental goal of education and of life itself is that a rational creature should so master his instruments of motion that his actions are not simply guided by an instinctive response to sense stimuli but also by reason itself. If an individual cannot attain this goal, he fails to attain that unity of personality to be expected in a rational animal.

17. THE INTELLIGENCE OF LOVE

Every work which is done according to the laws of nature and creates a harmony among beings attains consciousness under a form of love. This is, we may say, a sure sign of a creature's health and general well-being.

Love is not the cause but the effect. It is like a planet that receives its light from the sun. The moving force is instinct, the creative power of life; but in the process of creation it begets love, and this love fills the child's consciousness and affects his self-realization.

That irresistible impulse which unites a child with the objects about him during the sensitive periods is actually a love for his environment. It is not simply an emotional reaction, but an intellectual desire or love which enables a child to see and hear and thus develop. A natural desire which children have to observe can be called in Dante's words "the intelligence of love."

It is love that enables a child to observe in a keen and ardent fashion those features of his environment which are quite significant to adults because they lack a child's animation. Does not love make us sensible to things which are not noticed by others? Does it not reveal to us details and special qualities that are not appreciated by others? Because he is in love with his environment and not indifferent to it, a child's intelligence can see what is invisible to adults.

A child's love of his surroundings appears to adults as the natural joy and vivacity of youth. But they do not recognize it as a spiritual energy, a moral beauty which accompanies creation.

A child's love is by nature simple. He loves in order

that he may receive impressions which will furnish him with means of growth.

The special object of a child's affection is the adult. He receives from the adult the material help he needs and earnestly asks him for those things he needs for his self-development. For the child, the adult is a kind of venerable being. From his lips, as from a spring, he draws the words he must learn to speak.

Through his actions an adult shows a child how men behave. A child begins to live his own life by imitating the adults with whom he comes in contact. The words and actions of an adult are so fascinating for a child that they can almost hypnotize him. A child can be so sensitive to an adult that the adult in a way comes to live and act in him. We can recall the incident of the child who placed his shoes on the bedspread. His subsequent acts revealed his natural obedience but also the power of suggestion. What an adult tells a child remains engraved on his mind as if it had been cut in marble. We can recall the reaction of the little girl whose mother had received the parcel with the scarf and horn. Since children are so eager to learn and so burning with love, an adult should carefully weigh all the words he speaks before them.

A child readily obeys an adult. But when an adult asks him to renounce those instincts that favor his development, he cannot obey. When an adult demands such a sacrifice to his own personal interests, it is like attempting to stop the building of a child's teeth when he is teething. A child's tantrums and rebellions are nothing more than aspects of a vital conflict between his creative impulses and his love for an adult who fails to understand his needs. When a child is disobedient or has a tantrum an adult should always call to mind the conflict and try to interpret it as a defense of some unknown vital activity necessary for the child's development.

We should remember that a child loves us and wants to obey. A child loves an adult beyond everything else, and yet the reverse is usually heard: "How those parents love their child!" or "How those teachers love their pupils!"

Further, it is said that children must be taught to love their mothers and fathers, their teachers and all men, and even plants and animals.

But who teaches them all this? Who can teach one how to love? Will it be the adult who calls all of his childish manifestations tantrums, and who only thinks of defending himself and his possessions from the child? Such a one cannot be a teacher of love since he does not possess that sensibility which we have called "the intelligence of love."

Instead, it is really the child who loves, who wants to feel an adult near him, and who delights in attracting attention to himself: "Look at me! Stay with me!"

In the evening he goes to bed, a child calls the person he loves and does not like to see him go. And when we go to dinner a child who is still being nursed would like to come along, not to eat but simply to be near so that he can watch us. Adults fail to appreciate this deep love of the child. But we should remember that the little child who loves us now so much will grow up and disappear. Who will then love us as this child loves us now? Who will call us when he goes to bed, saying affectionately: "Stay with me!" instead of bidding us an indifferent "Good night"? Who will wish so earnestly to stand near us while we eat, only to watch us? We defend ourselves against this love, and we shall never find another like it! And we say restlessly: "I don't have the time! I can't! I'm busy!" while deep down we are thinking: "You must correct children or you will end up being their slaves." We want to free ourselves from a child so that we can do what we please, so that we are not inconvenienced.

It is a terrible nuisance when a child goes in to wake up his father and mother in the morning. But what drives a child to go in search of his parents as soon as he gets up if it is not love? When a child bounces from his bed early, at the break of day, he goes to find his still sleeping parents as if to say: "Learn to live holily! It is already light! It is morning!" But a child goes to his parents not to teach them but only to see again those whom he loves.

The room is perhaps still dark, tightly shut, so that the

brilliance of the day will not disturb the sleepers. The child comes and touches his parents; the father and mother grumble: "How many times have we told you not to come early in the morning to wake us up?" "I did not wake you," he replies, "I only wanted to give you a kiss." In effect he says: "I did not wish to wake you from your sleep, I only wanted to arouse your spirit."

Yes, the love of a child is of utmost importance. Fathers and mothers fall asleep over everything and need a new being to rouse them and to re-animate them with a fresh and living energy that they no longer possess. They need a being who acts differently and who can say to them each morning: "Rise to another life! Learn to live better!"

Yes! To live better! To feel the breath of love!

Without children to assist them, men would degenerate. If an adult does not strive to renew himself, a hard crust begins to form around his heart which will eventually make him insensible. We are reminded of the Last Judgment, when Christ will turn to the damned, to those who while they were on earth never used the means at hand to renew themselves, and curse them saying:

"Depart from me, you cursed, for when I was sick you did not cure me!"

And they will answer:

"But when, Lord, did we ever see you sick?"

"Whenever you saw one that was poor or sick, it was I. Depart from me, you cursed, because I was in prison and you did not visit me."

"But, Lord, when were you ever in prison?"

"I was in each one that was in prison."

The dramatic pages of the Gospel bear witness to the fact that adults should console Christ hidden in the poor, in the condemned, and in the suffering. And if we apply this stirring scene to children we can see that Christ appears to men also under the guise of a child.

"I loved you. I came to wake you in the morning, and you rejected me!"

"But when, Lord, did you come to my house in the morning to wake me, and I rejected you?"

"When your child came to call you, it was I. When he begged you not to leave him, it was I!"

Fools! It was Christ who came to waken us and to teach us love! But we thought that it was only a childish whim and thus lost our hearts!

PART II

18. THE EDUCATION OF THE CHILD

We must wake up to the great reality that children have a psychic life whose delicate manifestations escape notice and whose pattern of activity can be unconsciously disrupted by adults.

An adult environment is not a suitable environment for children, but rather an aggregate of obstacles that strengthen their defenses, warp their attitudes, and expose them to adult suggestions. The psychology and the education of children have been studied from an adult rather than from a child's point of view. As a consequence, their conclusions must be radically reviewed. As we have already seen, every unusual response of a child furnishes us with a problem to be solved; and every tantrum is the exterior expression of some deep-rooted conflict which is not to be interpreted simply as a defensive mechanism against a hostile environment but a manifestation of a nobler trait seeking to reveal itself. A tantrum is like a storm that prevents the soul of the child from coming out of its hidden retreat and showing itself to the world.

It is obvious that all these camouflages conceal the true soul of the child. The whims, struggles, and deformations hide his efforts to realize himself, and prevent him from revealing his true personality. Behind these disturbing, outward manifestations, there must be an individual spiritual embryo that is developing according to a definite plan. Beneath these outward manifestations an unknown child lies hidden who must be freed. The most urgent task facing educators is to come to know this unknown child and to free it from all entanglements.

The essential difference between psychoanalytical research and this psychological study of the unknown child lies principally in the fact that the secret of an adult's subconsciousness is something that he represses within himself, whereas a child's secret is barely hidden by his environment. To assist an adult we must help him untangle a skein of complex adaptations that have been made over a long period of time. To assist a child we must provide him with an environment which will enable him to develop freely. A child is passing through a period of self-realization, and it is enough simply to open up the door for him. And, as a matter of fact, a being that is creating itself, that is passing from non-being to being, from potency to act, cannot at this stage of its existence be complicated. Since it is in the possession of an expanding energy it has no great difficulty in manifesting itself.

In an open environment, that is, in one that is suitable to his age, a child's psychic life should develop naturally and reveal its inner secret. Unless this principle is maintained, all later attempts at education will only lead one more deeply into an endless maze.

The new education has as its primary aim the discovery and freeing of the child. The first problem with which it is concerned is the child's very existence, and the second is that of providing him with the necessary aid as he advances toward maturity. This means that there must be a suitable environment for the child's growth. Obstacles must be reduced to a minimum and the surroundings should provide the necessary means for the exercise of those activities which develop a child's energies. Since adults are also a part of a child's environment, they should adapt themselves to his needs. They should not be an obstacle to a child's independent activities, nor should they carry out for him those activities by means of which a child reaches maturity.

What is most characteristic of our system of education is the emphasis that is placed upon the environment.

The role of the teacher in our schools has been an object of interest and discussion. By his passive attitude he removes from the children the obstacle that is created by his own activity and authority. The children can thus become active themselves. The teacher is satisfied when he sees them acting by themselves and making progress. Without attributing anything of this to himself he can be inspired with the thoughts of John the Baptist: "He must increase, but I must decrease."

A further characteristic of our system of teaching is respect for the child's personality carried to a point never reached before.

These three principles have been elaborated in institutions originally known as "Children's Homes" (*Case dei Bambini*), a name with family connotations.

This new system of education has been widely discussed, particularly with respect to the reversed roles of child and adult—the teacher without a desk, without authority, and almost without teaching, and the child, the center of activity, free to move about as he wills and to choose his own occupations. Some have regarded this as a kind of Utopia, and others simply as an exaggeration.

On the other hand, other innovations have been sympathetically received: objects proportioned to a child's body, bright and luminous rooms, low windows decked with flowers, and miniature pieces of furniture modeled after those in modern homes, small tables, small armchairs, pretty curtains, little cupboards that can be easily opened by the children containing various objects which they can use at will. All of these things have come to be regarded as practical improvements that contribute to a child's development, and I believe that the greater number of Children's Homes deliberately preserve this external character of cheerfulness and convenience as one of their principal features.

Now, after intensive studies and much experience in these matters, it may be useful to consider them again, and especially in their origins.

It would be wrong to imagine that actual observation of

children led us to the startling conclusion that they possess a hidden nature and that the intuition of such a truth then led us to conceive the idea of a special type of school and a special system of education. It is impossible to make an observation of something that is still unknown. It is impossible for one through a simple intuition to attribute two natures to a child and then attempt to demonstrate them experimentally. What is unknown should reveal itself through its own proper energies, and when it does no one is more incredulous than the one who first witnesses it. Like the rest of the world he rejects what is new, and as a consequence this hitherto unknown fact must insistently force itself upon him before it is finally seen, recognized, and enthusiastically accepted. The individual who is struck with the new light and finally embraces it becomes ardently enamored of it and consecrates his life to it. So great is his enthusiasm that he thinks that he is its creator, whereas he has simply been sensible to its manifestations. It is difficult for us to perceive something new, and even more difficult to persuade ourselves of the reality of our discovery, since it is precisely before what is new that the gates of our senses are shut. When we do make such a discovery, however, and recognize its truth we become like the merchant in the Gospel in search of precious pearls. When we find one of great price, we sell all that we have in order that we may buy it.

Our intellectual outlook might be compared to that of an aristocratic drawing room. The room is closed to strangers. In order to enter it one must be presented by another who is already known. One who is not thus introduced must beat down the closed door or enter by stealth. And when he finally gets in he creates a sensation. Volta must have looked upon the twitchings of the dead frog with mixed feelings of surprise and incredulity, but he persisted in his experiment and identified a function of electricity. At times a trivial incident can open up a new and boundless horizon. By nature man is an explorer, and it is only by the discovery of the seemingly insignificant details that he advances.

In physics and the science of medicine there are strict standards for the identification of new phenomena. A new discovery in these fields is the identification of previously unknown facts that may have been quite unsuspected. Such facts are objective and do not depend upon a person's intuition. There are two steps in the demonstration of such a fact. It must be isolated and studied under different conditions. It must then be reproduced and studied from various aspects to be certain that it is not simply an illusion but a tangible possession of real value. An example of an initial discovery of seemingly insignificant facts that have had tremendous consequences may be seen in the first Children's Home.

THE ORIGIN OF OUR METHOD

The following description of the origin of our system of education is taken from old notes which I jotted down at the time.

Who are you?

Our first school for small children between the ages of three and six was opened on January 6, 1907. As yet I had no special system of instruction. I had nothing more than fifty extremely poor, ragged, and obviously timid children, many of whom were weeping. Almost all were the offspring of illiterate parents who had entrusted them to my care.

A room had been set aside in the apartment house in which these children lived, and I was invited to take care of this place of refuge so that the children would not be left abandoned on the stairs, where they would dirty up the walls and be a source of annoyance.

For some undefinable reason I felt that a great work was about to begin and that it would prosper. It was the feast of the Epiphany, and the theme of the Mass and Office for the day seemed to be a kind of prophecy: "The earth was completely covered with darkness when the star appeared in the East whose splendor was to be a guide for the peoples."

Those present for the opening ceremonies were somewhat surprised and asked themselves: "Why does Miss Montessori make so much of a refuge for the poor?"

I began my work like a farmer who has set aside good seed and who is offered a fertile field in which to sow it. But it turned out otherwise. I had hardly scratched the clods when I found gold instead of grain: the clods hid a precious treasure. I was like Aladdin with the lamp in his hands, not knowing that it was a key to hidden treasures. At least my work for those children brought me a series of surprises.

I had done a considerable amount of work among children of subnormal intelligence and had used various objects to teach them with good results. It was reasonable to suppose that the means that had been successfully employed to help the feeble-minded and straighten out their way of thinking would also be of some use to those of normal intelligence. From these experiences certain principles of mental hygiene have been elaborated and presented as convincingly as possible for the use of others. But this does not alter the fact that the first effects produced by these means on normal children surprised me greatly and often left me quite incredulous.

The objects which I gave to these normal children had a different effect upon them than they had had upon the mentally deficient. When a normal child is attracted by an object he fixes his whole attention intently upon it and continues to work without a break in a remarkable state of concentration. After the child has finished his work, he appears satisfied, rested, and happy. It was this feeling of rest and satisfaction that I first read on those small, peaceful countenances and in those eyes gleaming with the contentment of a voluntary task completed. The objects which I gave the children were like the key to a clock, but with a significant difference. After it is wound a clock continues to run by itself, and after a child is given an object to use, he not only continues to work with it, but his efforts leave him mentally stronger and healthier than before. It took time to persuade me that this was not an illusion. After each new experience which proved that this was true, I remained for a long time in disbelief, but at the same time quite shaken and alarmed. How often it happened that I reproved the teacher when she told me what the children were doing! "Don't come to tell me such fantasies," I kept saying severely, and I remember that she, without being offended, would tearfully reply: "You are right. When I see such things I think that it must be the angels who are inspiring these children."

Finally, one day as I looked upon these children with great respect and affection, I placed my hand upon my heart and asked, "Who are you?" Were these perhaps the little children whom Christ had embraced and of whom he had said, "Whoever receives this little child for my sake, receives me," and again, "Whoever does not accept the kingdom of God as a little child will not enter into it."

This is how I came to meet them. They were tearful, frightened children, so timid that I could not get them to speak. Their faces were expressionless, their eyes bewildered as if they had never seen anything before in their lives. They were in fact poor, neglected children who had been reared in dark, decrepit homes without anything to stimulate their minds. Anyone could have seen that they were undernourished, that they needed to be fed and exposed to the open air and sun. They were like buds that seemed never destined to bloom.

What were the peculiar circumstances that produced such a striking transformation? What was it that gave them a new life whose radiance has spread throughout the whole world?

The obstacles to their development were obviously removed and means found to free their souls. But who could have imagined what these obstacles were, or who could have guessed what was needed to enable the souls of these children to burgeon and flower? Frequently it was something that might seem to have been destined to produce the opposite effect.

We can begin with the family background of these children. Their parents belonged to the lowest strata of society. Almost all of them were illiterate. They had no regular employment but had to seek work day by day, and thus had neither the time nor the means to take proper care of their children.

There was obviously no future in caring for such charges. Since it was impossible to find a trained teacher for the children, a young working-woman was hired to take care of them. She had once studied to become a teacher but had given it up, and as a consequence had neither the education nor the prejudices that would otherwise have been hers. Another factor to be taken into account was that our first school was a private undertaking. It was sponsored by a real estate company which wrote off its support as an indirect expense incurred in the maintenance of the building. The children were simply brought together to keep them from damaging the walls of the tenement, and thus diminish the cost of repairs. It was not a true social work. There was no thought of anything like free meals for the children or medical care for the sick. The funds provided were simply those that would be required for the setting up of an office with furniture and other equipment. This is why we began to make our own tables and chairs instead of buying regular school desks. If it had not been for these various circumstances, we would not have been able to isolate and demonstrate the various psychological factors that brought about the transformation of these children.

The first Children's Home was thus not so much a school as a yardstick whose usefulness was yet unknown. Since our funds were so limited there were no desks for children or teacher, or any of the other usual equipment found in ordinary schools. The room was simply furnished as if it were an office or a home. But despite the simplicity of the surroundings I did have some special equipment made like that which I had used in an institute for defective children. This, however, would certainly not have been classified as school equipment. The first Children's Home was not bright and cheerful like those we see today. There was a stout table that served more or less as the teacher's desk and a massive cabinet in which different objects could be stored. Its solid doors were locked with keys entrusted to the teacher. The children's tables were built for strength and durability. They were placed one behind the other like desks in a school and were long enough for three children to sit at them in a row. Besides stools for the children there were simple little armchairs for each child. There were no flowers, which later became characteristic of our schools, since the courtyard, though it was cultivated, contained nothing but patches of lawn and trees. I had no illusions that I could make any important experiments in such a school. Nevertheless I set to work at training the senses of the children to see if there was any difference between their reactions and those of the subnormal children with whom I had worked before. I was particularly interested in seeing if there was any difference between the actions of normal children of tender age and those of older but mentally deficient children.

I placed no restrictions upon the teacher and imposed no special duties. I merely showed her how to use the various objects for training the children's senses so that she could instruct the children in their use. She became interested in the material, but I did not prevent her from using her own initiative.

After a little time I discovered that the teacher had herself made other objects for the children's use. Among these were decorated gold crosses. She made these out of paper and passed them out as rewards for good behavior. I often found one or other of the children wearing these harmless pendants. On her own initiative she also taught them how to make a military salute, holding one hand to their breasts while touching their foreheads with the other. These salutes seemed to please her and I found them as harmless as they were amusing, since the oldest of the children was only five.

In such circumstances, then, we began our life of peace and isolation. For a long time no one noticed what we were doing. It may be useful, however, to summarize the principle events of this period. My own interventions were anything but scientific, and what occurred may seem to be quite insignificant. Nevertheless, some important observations and discoveries were being made.

19. OBSERVATIONS AND DISCOVERIES

REPETITION OF THE EXERCISE

The first thing I particularly noticed was a little girl of about three busy slipping cylinders in and out of their containers. These cylinders are of different sizes and have corresponding holes into which they fit like a cork in a bottle. I was surprised to see so small a child performing this exercise over and over again with such intense interest. She showed no apparent increase in speed or facility in executing the task: it was a kind of perpetual motion. From force of habit I began to count the number of times she repeated the exercise. I then decided to see how concentrated she was in her strange employment. I told the teacher to make the other children sing and move about. But this did not disturb the child at all in her labors. I then gently picked up the chair in which she was sitting and set it on top of a small table. As I lifted the chair she clutched the objects with which she was working and placed them on her knees, but then continued with the same task. From the time I began to count, she repeated the exercise forty-two times. Then she stopped as if coming out of a dream and smiled happily. Her eyes shone brightly and she looked about. She had not even noticed what we had done to disturb her. And now, for no apparent reason, her task was finished. But what was finished and why?

This gave us our first insight into the unexplored depths of a child's mind. This little girl was at an age when attention is fickle, when the mind skips from one thing to another without being able to stop. And yet she had become so absorbed in what she was doing that her ego became insensible to external stimuli. Her concentration had been accompanied by a rhythmical movement of her hands as she fitted the different objects together.

Similar events kept recurring, and every time children emerged from such an experience, they were like individuals who had rested. They were filled with life and resembled those who have experienced some great joy.

Though periods of concentration that made the children oblivious to the outer world were not frequent, I noted a strange behavior that was common to all and nearly constant in all their actions. This was what I later called "repetition of the exercise."

One day, as I watched their dirty little hands at work, I thought I would teach the children something useful—how to wash their hands. I then noticed that the children continued to wash them even after they were clean. When they left the school they would wash them again. Some mothers told me that in the morning they would find their children in the laundry washing their hands. Some were even so proud of showing off their clean hands that on one occasion they were taken for little beggars. They repeated the exercise again and again for no external reason. This frequently happened in other activities as well, and the more carefully an exercise was taught in all its details the more it became an object of endless repetition.

FREE CHOICE

Another very simple truth also came to light. The children used objects distributed to them by the teacher, who later returned them to their proper place. She told me that whenever she collected these objects, the children got up from their seats and came near to her. No matter how often she sent them back they always returned. She had therefore concluded that the children were disobedient.

As I watched them, I realized that they wished to put the objects back where they belonged. I let them do it, and this began a new kind of life for them; they were enthralled with putting things in order and straightening them up. If a glass of water slipped from a child's hands, others would run up to collect the broken pieces and wipe the floor.

One day the teacher dropped a box containing about eighty little squares of different graded colors. I remember her embarrassment since it was difficult to sort out so many different shades. But at this point the children ran up and, to our great amazement, quickly arranged them in to their proper order, showing in this a wonderful sensitivity that was superior to our own.

One day the teacher came a bit late to school after having forgotten to lock the cupboard. She found that the children had opened its door. Many of them were standing about it, while others were removing objects and carrying them away. The teacher considered this a kind of theft and believed that children who were so lacking in respect for school and teacher as to steal should be treated with severity and be given some moral principles to guide them. I, on the other hand, interpreted the incident as a sign that the children now knew the objects so well that they could make their own choice, and this proved to be the case.

This began a new and interesting activity for the children. They could now choose their own occupations according to their own particular preferences. From this time on we made use of low cupboards so that the children could take from them the material that corresponded to their own inner needs. The principle of *free choice* was thus added to that of *repetition of the exercise*.

The free choices made by the children enabled us to observe their psychic needs and tendencies. One of the first interesting discoveries was that the children did not choose all the various objects provided for them but only certain ones. They almost always went to choose the same things, and some with an obvious preference. Other objects were neglected and became covered with dust.

I would show them all to the children and had the

teacher distribute them and explain their use, but the children would not take some of them up again of their own accord.

I then came to realize that everything about a child should not only be in order, but that it should be *proportioned to the child's use,* and that interest and concentration arise specifically from the elimination of what is confusing and superfluous.

TOYS

Although the children in our first school could play with some really splendid toys, none cared to dc so. This surprised me so much that I decided to help them play with their toys, showing them how to handle the tiny dishes, lighting the fire in the doll's kitchen, and placing near it a pretty doll. The children were momentarily interested but then went off on their own. Since they never freely chose these toys, I realized that in the life of a child play is perhaps something of little importance which he undertakes for the lack of something better to do. A child feels that he has something of greater moment to do than to be engaged in such trivial occupations. He regards play as we would regard a game of chess or bridge. These are pleasant occupations for hours of leisure, but they would become painful if we were obliged to pursue them at greath length. When we have some important business to do, bridge is forgotten. And since a child always has some important thing at hand, he is not particularly interested in playing.

Because a child is constantly passing from a lower to a higher state, his every passing minute is precious. Since a child is constantly growing, he is fascinated by everything that contributes to his development and becomes indifferent to idle occupations.

REWARDS AND PUNISHMENTS

Once I entered the school and saw a child sitting in an

THE MONTESSORI ENVIRONMENT

Little Flower Montessori Program—South Bend, Indiana

The environment is the center of instruction in the Montessori method. The practical life area is one of four general areas in this prepared environment. Activities here build on the child's natural interest and help him develop good work habits, concentration, eye-hand coordination, a lengthened attention span and control of his body. The tire washing exercise, like tabletop washing, uses a circular motion that will be a base for later hand exercises such as drawing and writing. The pouring exercise and other kitchen work helps develop control of self and mastery of the environment.

Convent of the Visitation—St. Paul, Minnesota

The sensorial area. Since "nothing comes to the intellect that is not first in the senses," the Montessori environment provides a wide range of sensorial materials designed to help the child develop his ability to make judgments, to compare and discriminate on the basis of size, shape, weight, texture, color and temperature; to store up impressions in his "muscular memory," and to develop the use of certain muscles and certain motions. There are jars to be sniffed for their aromas, sound cylinders to be listened to, color tablets to be arranged in gradation, block towers to be built and knobbed cylinders to be put in their places.

Oak Park Montessori School—Oak Park, Illinois

Alcuin Montessori School—Oak Park, Illinois

Oak Park Montessori School—Oak Park, Illinois

Convent of the Visitation—St. Paul, Minnesota

In the language area, tracing the outline of metal insets such as the quadrafoil shown here prepares the hand and arm muscles for drawing and writing.

Working with the individual letters of the movable alphabet, the child can match these with the sandpaper letters, tracing their shape on the sandpaper with his fingers thus reinforcing his visual recognition of the letters. Using small pictures the child will then sound out and construct words with the letters.

Oak Park Montessori School—Oak Park, Illinois

Convent of the Visitation
—St. Paul, Minnesota

Convent of the Visitation—St. Paul, Minnesota

In the math area, materials such as the numerical rods enable the child to get a physical sense of quantity and then to associate this with the numeral that is the symbol for that quantity. The spindle box gives them a chance to reinforce this skill, counting from zero to nine, and introduces the concept of sets. The decimal beads lets them build up to the quantity of 1000 in a visible way and to learn the value of place.

Alcuin Montessori School—Oak Park, Illinois

A part of the normalizing process is to help the child understand and be comfortable with the things of nature. Working with growing things—planting bulbs, collecting and identifying leaves, as these children in an elementary program are doing—is an important part of the extended Montessori environment. In music, the Orff instruments are a natural complement to the Montessori materials.

Little Flower Montessori Program—South Bend, Indiana

armchair all by himself in the center of the room with nothing to do. He was wearing on his breast one of the decorations which the teacher gave out for good behavior. She told me, however, that the little fellow was being punished. Another child had received the reward and had placed it on his own breast, but then had given it to the one being punished as if it were something useless and a hindrance to one who wanted to work.

The child in the armchair looked indifferently at the badge and then gazed calmly about the room, quite oblivious to any sense of shame. This single incident made us realize the futility of rewards and punishments, but we made further observations in greater detail. Long experience only confirmed our first intuition. The teacher even reached a state where she felt ashamed to reward or punish children who seemed equally indifferent to either treatment. What was even more surprising was their frequent refusal of a reward. This marked an awakening in the conscience of a sense of dignity that had not previously existed.

Eventually we gave up either punishing or rewarding the children.

SILENCE

One day I entered the classroom holding in my arms a four-month-old baby girl that I had taken from her mother in the courtyard. The infant was tightly wrapped in swaddling bands as was the custom among the people of this neighborhood. Her face was full and rosy. She was so still that her silence impressed me greatly and I wanted the children to share my feelings. "She is not making a sound," I told them. And jokingly I added, "None of you could do so well." To my great surprise I saw that the children were looking at me with an extraordinary intensity. They seemed to be hanging on my lips and to be feeling keenly what I was saying. "Notice," I continued, "how soft her breath is. None of you could breath as silently as she." Surprised and motionless, the children began to hold their breaths. At that moment there impressive silence. The tick-tock of the clock, which was not usually heard, began to become audible. It seemed as if the little girl had brought an atmosphere of silence into the room which is never found in daily life.

No one made the least perceptible movement. They were intent upon experiencing the silence and reproducing it. All the children lent themselves to the task, not it must be said with enthusiasm, since enthusiasm implies something that is impulsive and openly manifest. But here was something that rose up from a deep desire. The children all sat perfectly still breathing as quietly as possible, having on their faces a serene and intent expression like those who are meditating. Little by little in the midst of this impressive silence we could all hear the lightest sounds like that of a drop of water falling in the distance and the far-off chirping of a bird.

This was the origin of our *exercise of silence*.

One day it occurred to me that I could use this silence to test the sharpness of the children's hearing. From a little distance I began to call them by name in a whisper. Whoever heard his name had to come to me, walking in such a way as to make no sound. I thought that an exercise of such patient waiting would be a trial for the children, so I brought with me bits of candy and chocolates to reward the children as they came up. But they refused the sweets. It seemed almost as if they were saying, "Do not spoil this beautiful experience. Our minds are still elated. Do not distract us."

I thus came to understand that children are not only sensitive to silence but also to a voice that calls them almost inaudibly out of that silence. They will come up slowly walking on tiptoes and taking care not to knock against anything that would make them heard.

I later came to realize that every exercise involving movement where mistakes can be corrected, as in this case where noise was checked by silence, is of great assitance to a child. Repetition of such an exercise can lead a child to perform exterior acts with a perfection which it could never attain through mere instruction.

Our children became agile and alert by learning how to walk around various objects without bumping into them and how to run lightly without making a sound. They rejoiced in the perfection with which they performed such actions. They were interested in discovering their potentialities and in exercising themselves in the mysterious world where their lives were unfolding.

It was a long time before I persuaded myself that there was an intrinsic reason behind the children's refusal of candy. This refusal seemed so extraordinary to me, since children are notoriously eager for sweets, that I decided to make a further test. I brought some candy to school with me, but the children refused it or put it in the pockets of their smocks. Since they were all very poor, I thought that they perhaps wanted to take the candy back to their homes. "The pieces I gave you," I told them, "you can take home, but these are for you." They took the candy but again put it in their pockets without eating it. They appreciated the gift, however, as was discovered when their teacher visited one of the children that was sick. The little boy was so grateful for her coming that he opened up a small box and took out a large piece of candy which he had received at school and offered it to her. The tempting sweet had remained there for several weeks and the child had not touched it. This attitude was so common among the children that many visitors later came to our schools simply to verify this phenomenon which they had read about in different books. It was a spontaneous and natural development within the children. No one would have thought of teaching them to practice penance and to forgo sweets, or have been so unrealistic as to say, "Children should neither play nor eat candy." Of their own accord the children refused these useless, exterior delights as they rose higher in the spiritual life. One day a person gave them cookies that had been baked in geometrical shapes. Instead of eating them, the children looked intently at them and said, "Here is a circle! Here is a rectangle!" An amusing story is told about the child of poor parents who was watching his mother in the kitchen. She picked up a chunk of butter, and the child said, "It's a rectangle!" His mother cut off a corner and the child said, "Now you have a traingle," and he added, "What's left is a trapezoid." And he never said what might have been expected, "Give me some bread and butter."

DIGNITY

One day I decided to give the children a slightly humorous lesson on how to blow their noses. After I had shown them different ways to use a handkerchief, I ended by indicating how it could be done as unobtrusively as possible. I took out my handkerchief in such a way that they could hardly see it and blew my nose as softly as I could. The children watched me in rapt attention, but failed to laugh. I wondered why, but I had hardly finished my demonstration when they broke out into applause that resembled a long repressed ovation in a theater. I had never heard such tiny hands make so much noise, and I had no idea that such small children would applaud so enthusiastically. It then occurred to me that I had perhaps touched a sensitive spot in their little social world. Children have a particular difficulty in blowing their noses. Since they are constantly being scolded on this score, they are sensitive about it. The shouts they hear and the insulting epithets that are hurled at them hurt their feelings. And insult is added to injury when they finally end up wearing at school a handkerchief blatantly pinned to their smocks so that they will not lose it. But no one really teaches them how they should blow their noses. When I tried to do so, they felt compensated for past humiliations, and their applause indicated that I had not only treated them with justice but had enabled them to get a new standing in society.

Long experience has taught me that this is a proper interpretation of the incident. I have come to appreciate the fact that children have a deep sense of personal dignity. Adults, as a rule, have no concept of how easily they are wounded and oppressed.

On that particular day when I was on the point of leaving the school, the children began to shout, "Thank you, thank you for the lesson!" When I left the building they followed me in a silent procession until I finally told them: "When you go back, run on tiptoe and take care that you don't bump into the corner of the wall." They turned around and disappeared behind the gate as if they were flying. I had touched these poor little children to the quick.

When visitors came to the school, the children behaved with dignity and self-respect. They knew how to receive these visitors with warm enthusiasm and show them how they carried out their tasks.

Once we were warned that an important individual wanted to be left alone with the children so that he could observe them by himself. I told the teacher: "Simply let things go as they will." And turning to the children, I added: "You are going to have a visitor tomorrow. I would like him to think that you are the best children in the world." I later asked the teacher how the visit had turned out. "It was a great success," she replied. "Some of the children offered the visitor a chair and said politely: 'Please be seated.' Others said: 'Good day.' And when he left, they leaned out of the windows and called out: 'Thank you for your visit, come again!' " "But why," I asked, "did you take such aims to instruct them? I told you not to do anything unusual but simply to let the children act as they pleased." "But I didn't tell the children anything," she replied, and then went on to explain that the children had worked more diligently than usual with their different projects. Everything had gone marvelously well to the great surprise and edification of the visitor.

For some time I was skeptical about what the teacher had told me. I feared that she had perhaps given some special instructions to the children, and I questioned her again about this. But I at last saw the light. The children had acquired a sense of their own dignity. They respected their visitors and were proud to show them what they could do. Had I not told them, "I would like your visitors to think you are the best children in the world"? But it was certainly not my exhortation that made them act as they did. Whenever I told them, "You will have a visitor," it was like announcing the arrival of a guest in a drawing room. These poised little children, full of charm and dignity, were always ready to receive visitors. They had lost their former timidity. There was now no obstacle lying between their souls and their surroundings. Their lives were unfolding naturally like the lotus that spreads out its white petals to receive the rays of the sun as it sends forth a fragrant odor. The important thing was that the children found no obstacles in the way to their development. They had nothing to hide, nothing to fear, nothing to shun. It was as simple as that. Their self-possession could be attributed to their immediate and perfect adaptation to their environment.

The children were alert, active, but always composed, radiating a spiritual warmth that cheered the hearts of the adults who came in contact with them. Many persons began to visit them to experience this for themselves and they were all received with affection.

It was interesting to see the reactions produced by these visits. Elegantly dressed women wearing their jewels as if they were going to a reception relished the unspoiled admiration of the children and were delighted by the way in which the children expressed their wonder.

They stroked the beautiful cloth of the ladies' dresses and caressed their soft perfumed hands. Once a child approached a woman who was in mourning and leaned his little head against her, then he took one of her hands and held it between his own. She later observed with much emotion that no one had given her so much comfort as those little children.

One day the daughter of the Prime Minister accompanied the ambassador of the Republic of Argentina in a visit to the Children's Home. The ambassador had been advised not to give any notice of his intended visit so that he might witness the children's spontaneity of which he had often heard. When they arrived at the school, however, they learned that it was closed because it was a holiday. Some children in the courtyard then came up, and one of them explained with perfect naturalness, "It makes no difference that this is a holiday. We are all here in the building and the porter has the key." Then the children began to run about and call their comrades by name. The door of the classroom was opened and they all set to work. Their marvelous spontaneity was proved beyond question.

The children's mothers appreciated what was happening and came to tell me what was occurring within the family circle. "These little children of three or four," they would confidentially report, "tell us things that would offend us if they were not our children. They say for example: 'Your hands are dirty, you should wash them,' or 'You should clean those stains off of your clothes.' When we hear them saying such things to us, we are not offended. Their warnings come to us as if in a dream."

Actually, these poor people became cleaner and tidier. Broken pots began to disappear from the window sills. Window panes began to sparkle and geraniums began to blossom in the windows facing the courtyard.

DISCIPLINE

Despite their easy freedom of manner, the children on the whole gave the impression of being extraordinarily disciplined. They worked quietly, each one intent on his own particular occupation. They quietly walked to and fro as they took or replaced the objects with which they worked. They would leave the classroom, take a look at the courtyard and then return. They carried out their teacher's bidding with surprising rapidity. She told me: "They do so exactly what I tell them that I am beginning to feel responsible for every word I say."

As a matter of fact, if she wanted them, for example, to perform the exercise of silence, the children would be motionless before she could finish the request. This apparent dependence did not, however, hinder them from acting on their own, arranging their day as they pleased. They would take the objects they wanted for their work, and tidy up the school. If the teacher came late or left the children alone, everything went on just as well. What particularly fascinated visitors was the order and discipline they managed to combine with spontaneity.

What was the source of the perfect discipline that informed them even in periods of intense silence and of the obedience that almost anticipated the orders given?

The peaceful atmosphere that pervaded the classroom as the children pursued their work was extremely touching. No one had provoked it, and no one could have obtained it by external means.

WRITING AND READING

One day two or three mothers came to me and asked me to teach their children how to read and write. The women were themselves illiterate and were making the request in their own name and that of others. When I objected that such an undertaking was something more than I had in mind, they persisted in their entreaties.

This marked the beginning of a number of surprises. All that I taught these four- or five-year-old children were some letters of the alphabet which I had the teacher cut out of cardboard. Some of these were made out of sandpaper so that the children could run their fingers over them and feel their shape. I placed these on boards, grouping letters of a similar shape together so that the hands of the children as they touched them would follow somewhat the same motions. The teacher was satisfied with this arrangement and did nothing more to help the children.

We failed to understand why the children were so enthusiastic. They would march around in procession holding up the letters of the alphabet like banners and uttering shouts of joy. But why?

One day I surprised a little boy who was walking by

himself and repeating: "To make Sofia, you have to have an 'S,' an 'O,' an 'F,' an 'I,' and an 'A,'" and with this he repeated the sounds making up the word. He was thus engaged in a study and analysis of a word he had in mind and was looking for its component sounds. With the keen interest of one making a discovery he was coming to understand that each of these sounds corresponded to a letter of the alphabet. And, as a matter of fact, what is phonetic spelling except a correspondence between sound and sign? Language is primarily something that is spoken; its written counterpart is only a literal transfer of the sounds into visible signs. Progress in writing is marked by the parallel development of the written and spoken languages. In the beginning, a written language is distilled from its spoken counterpart like separate drops that eventually run together to form a distinct stream of written words and sentences.

Writing is a key to a double gain. It enables the hand to master a vital skill like that of speaking and to create a second means of communication that reflects the spoken word in all its details. Writing is thus dependent upon mind and hand.

Writing should logically flow as a natural consequence of the development of a fixed alphabet. To write properly, however, the hand must be able to draw signs. The signs of the alphabet are as a rule easy to draw since they represent nothing but particularized sounds. But I had not thought of all this before the children taught themselves to write.

This was the greatest event to take place in the first Children's Home. The child who first made the discovery was so astonished that he shouted out loud: "I've written, I've written!" The children excitedly ran up to look at the words which he had traced on the floor with a piece of chalk. "Me too, me too!" they shouted as they ran off in search of writing materials. Some crowded around the blackboard. Others stretched themselves out upon the floor. They all began to write.

Their boundless activity was like a torrent. They wrote

everywhere, on doors, walls, and even on loaves of bread at home. The children were only about four years old, and their discovery of writing had been totally unforeseen. The teacher told me: "It was three o'clock yesterday when the little boy began to write."

We were struck as if we had witnessed a miracle. We had earlier received some beautifully illustrated books, but when we now gave them to the children, they received them coolly. They contained beautiful pictures, it was true, but these only distracted them from the new and enthralling occupation that absorbed their energies. They wanted to write and not to look at pictures. The children had perhaps never before seen books, and for a long time we tried to arouse their interest in them, but it was even impossible to make them understand what we meant by reading. We therefore set the books aside, waiting for a more favorable time. The children were rarely interested in reading what another had written. It even seemed that they were unable to read the words. Many of the children would turn around and look at me in amazement when I read out loud the words they had written, as if to ask, "How do you know it?"

It was only after some six months that they began to understand what it is to read, and they did this only by associating reading with writing. They watched my hand as I traced letters on a piece of white paper and came to realize that I was communicating my thoughts as if I were speaking. As soon as this was clear to them, they began to take the pieces of paper on which I had written something and carry them off to a corner and try to read them. They did this mentally without pronouncing the words. One could tell when they understood the writing by the smiles which would suddenly spread across their faces that had been then contracted with effort and by the little jumps of joy as if some hidden spring within them had suddenly been released. Each of the sentences I wrote contained an "order" that I could have given by word of mouth: "Open the window," "Come near me," and the like. This is how they began to read. They eventually progressed to the point where they could read long sentences containing complicated commands. But it seemed that writing was understood by the children simply as another way of expressing oneself, another form of speech which, like speech itself, was passed directly from one person to another.

Indeed, when visitors came, many of the children who earlier had been almost too vocal in their greetings now remained silent. They would rise and go to write on the blackboard: "Please sit down," "Thank you for your visit," and the like.

One day we were talking of a great disaster that had occurred in Sicily: an earthquake had completely destroyed the city of Messina causing thousands of deaths. A child of about five got up, went to the blackboard, and began to write: "I am sorry . . ." We watched him expecting that he would express his sorrow for what had happened. Instead he continued: "I am sorry that I am small." This was certainly a strange observation, but the little fellow went on: "If I were big, I would go to help." He had written a little essay that revealed his innate goodness. He was the son of a woman who supported him by selling herbs on the streets.

There was a further surprise in store for us. While we were preparing material to teach the Roman alphabet to the children so that we could make another attempt with the books, the children began to read all the print that they found in the school. And there were some things that were really difficult to decipher, such as a calendar on which the words were printed in Gothic type. During this same time the children's parents came to say that they stopped in the streets to read the signs of the shops and that it was impossible to go for a walk with them. It was evident that the children were more interested in figuring out the letters of the alphabet than in reading the words. They would see a different kind of writing and learn to read it from the meaning of a word. It was an intuitional process like that used by adults in deciphering prehistoric writings carved on rock. The meaning they find in the symbols is a proof that they have deciphered them.

If we had been in too great a hurry to explain the printed characters to the children, we would have quenched their interest and eager insight. A premature insistence upon their reading words from books would have had a negative effect. The pursuit of this less important good would have diminished the energies of their dynamic minds. The books, as a consequence, remained for a long time in the cupboard. Only later were the children put into contact with them. It began in an interesting manner. A child came to school one day highly excited. He was hiding in his hand a piece of crumpled paper, and he confided to one of his comrades: "Guess what is in this piece of paper." "There's nothing on it; it is only a torn piece of paper." "No, there is a story." "A story on it?" This attracted a crowd of curious children. The child had picked up a page of a book from a rubbish heap, and he began to read it, to read a story.

Then they understood the meaning of a book, and books became objects of great demand. Many of the children, however, when they found something interesting to read tore out the page and carried it away. Those poor books! The discovery of their value was truly disconcerting. The usually peaceful order of the school was disrupted, and we had to check those eager little hands that had become destructive through their love of reading. Even before they read from books and learned to respect them, the children with some help on our part had learned to spell and to write so perfectly that they were compared with children in the third grade in grammar schools.

PHYSICAL EFFECTS

During all this time nothing had been done to improve the children's health. But now no one would have recognized in their rosy and vivacious countenances the undernourished, anemic children that had seemed to be so much in need of food, tonics, and medical care. They were physically as well as if they had been cured by exposure to fresh air and the healing rays of the sun.

Indeed, if psychic impressions can have an influence on the metabolism and thus lower one's vitality, the opposite can also happen: a stimulating psychic experience can increase the rate of metabolism and thus contribute to one's physical well-being. Our work with these children was a proof of this. Today, when this truth is generally accepted, our experiences would not make much of an impression, but at the time they created a sensation.

Men spoke of "miracles," and reports on these wonderful children spread like wildfire. The press spoke of them in glowing terms. Books and even novels were written about them. Though their authors gave an exact account of what they had seen, they seemed to be describing a different world. Men spoke of the discovery of the human soul. They even quoted the children's conversations. A book was written about them in England called *The New Children*. Many people came, especially from America, to verify what they had read.

20. THE "METHOD"

This brief account of incidents and impressions leaves open the problem of method. What method was used to obtain these results? This is a question of considerable importance.

There was no method to be seen, what was seen was a child. A child's soul freed from impediments was seen acting according to its own nature. The characteristics of childhood which we isolated belong quite simply to the life of a child, just as colors belong to a bird and fragrances to flowers. They are not at all the product of an "educational method." It should, however, be obvious that education can have an influence upon these natural qualities by protecting them and nurturing them in a way that will assist their natural development.

We see a parallel for this in the cultivation of new strains of flowers. With proper care and treatment horticulturalists can improve their scents, colors, and other natural qualities.

In the Children's Home we were able to observe natural psychic traits. These are not as apparent as the physiological traits of plants. A child's psychic life is so fluid that its natural manifestations can completely disappear in an unfavorable environment and be replaced by others. Before elaborating any system of education, we must therefore create a favorable environment that will encourage the flowering of a child's natural gifts. All that is needed is to remove the obstacles. And this should be the basis of, and point of departure for, all future education.

The first thing to be done, therefore, is to discover the

true nature of a child and then assist him in his normal development.

If we examine the special circumstances that accidentally occasioned the flowering of these children's normal traits, we can recognize some of particular importance. The first of these was the pleasant environment in which the children were placed and where they were left pretty much to their own resources. The clean, white classroom with its new little tables, its small stools and tiny armchairs made especially for them, and the grassy spots in the courtyard warmed by the sun must have been extremely attractive to those poor children who had come from such miserable homes. A second favorable condition was the neutral character of the adults. Their parents were illiterate, their teacher an ordinary working woman without ambition and without preconceptions. This led to a kind of intellectual calm.

It has always been recognized that a teacher must be *calm,* but this calmness is usually considered to be one of character, a lack of nervousness. But there is here a question of a deeper calm, an empty, or better, unencumbered state that is a source of inner clarity. This calm consists in a spiritual humility and intellectual purity necessary for the understanding of a child, and which, as a consequence, must be found in a teacher.

Another important circumstance was the fact that the children were given special material with which to work. They were attracted by these objects which perfected their sense perceptions, enabling them to analyze and facilitate their movements. These materials also taught them how to concentrate in a way that no vocal instruction ever could have done.

From this we can see that the special circumstances surrounding the children were a suitable environment, a humble teacher, and material objects adapted to their needs.

We can now describe some of the ways in which children respond to these external influences. The most striking, and one that is almost like a magic wand for opening the gate to the normal expression of a child's natural gifts, is activity concentrated on some task that requires movement of the hands guided by the intellect. This gives rise to further activities more deeply rooted in the child's interior such as a "repetition of the exercise," and "free choice." These reveal the true child. We see him kindled with joy and indefatigable in his toil since his activities are like a psychic metabolism with which his life and growth are intimately connected. Choice is now his guiding principle. He enthusiastically responds to various tests like that of silence. He is enthralled with certain lessons that point out the path of honor and justice. He eagerly assimilates means that enable him to develop his mind. But he turns from other things such as prizes, toys, and candy. He further shows us that he has a need of order and discipline as mirrors of his inner life. And yet he is still a child, fresh, gay, sincere, and lively. He shouts with joy and claps his hands. He runs about and greets others with a loud voice. He is generous with his thanks and shows his gratitude by calling to, and running after, his benefactor. He is friendly with everyone, admires what he sees, and adapts himself to everything.

We can draw up a list of his preferences and of the ways in which he spontaneously manifests himself. And we can add to this what he rejects as a waste of time.

1. *What he likes*
Repetition of the exercise.
Free choice.
Control of error.
Analysis of movements.
Exercise of silence.
Good manners in social contacts.
Order in the environment.
Care for personal cleanliness.
Training of the senses.
Writing separated from reading.
Writing before reading.
Reading without books.
Discipline in free activity.

2. *What he rejects*

Rewards and punishments.

Spellers.

Lessons in common.*

Programs and examinations.

Toys and sweets.

A teacher's desk.

In these lists we can, of course, find an outline of a system of education. Children themselves have furnished us with practical, positive, and tested norms for constructing an educational system in which their own choices are a guiding principle and their natural vivacity prevents mistakes.

These principles have been retained intact throughout the subsequent elaboration of our system of education. They remind us of the embryo of a vertebrate. In it may be seen a shadowy line that will become the spinal column. Within the line may be seen spots which will develop into the separate vertebrae. The embryo itself is divided into three parts representing the head, chest, and abdomen. Similarly, the basic outline of our educational system had a linear unity marked with a number of individual features which developed like the vertebrae, and the whole was divided into three different areas comprising environment, teacher, and the various objects used by the children.

It would be interesting to trace the evolution of this original outline step by step. We could thus see how a primitive insight has developed into a concept of great importance for human society. The successive developments of this particular method of education may be described as evolutionary since what is new in it comes from a life that is unfolding with respect to its environ-

* This does not mean that in Children's Homes there are no lessons in common but rather that these are not the only, or even the chief means of instruction. Common lessons are used simply as introductions to special problems and activities.

ment. The environment itself is moreover something special. Though it is provided by adults, it is in reality an active and vital response to the new patterns manifested in the life of a growing child.

The extraordinary rapidity with which this system of education has been adopted for children of every race and every social condition has provided us with an abundance of experimental data and enabled us to identify common features and universal tendencies and thus to determine the natural laws upon which the education of children should be based.

The first schools that developed from the original Children's Home are particularly interesting in that they retained the practice of waiting for the spontaneous reactions of the children before any further exterior norms were adopted.

A striking example of this may be found in the establishment of one of the first Children's Homes in Rome. The circumstances of its origin were even stranger than those of our first school since it was established to take care of orphaned children who had lived through one of the greatest disasters of history, the earthquake at Messina. Some sixty of these little tots were found alone among the ruins. No one knew their names or their social conditions. A terrible shock had made them all very much alike, depressed, silent, indifferent. They were hard to feed and to put asleep. At night they could be heard crying and weeping. The queen of Italy became greatly interested in these unfortunates and a delightful place was set aside for them. Their new home contained bright and attractive pieces of furniture accommodated to their size. There were little cabinets with doors, low round tables painted in bright colors, somewhat higher rectangular tables, stools and armchairs. The windows were hung with colored curtains. The children had their own little knives, forks, spoons, plates, napkins, and even pieces of soap and towels the right size for their little hands. There were pictures on the walls and vases of flowers placed about the rooms. The site that had been chosen for these unfortunate children was a convent of Franciscan nuns with spacious gardens, wide paths, pools of goldfish, and beautiful beds of flowers. In these surroundings the sisters in their grey robes and long majestic veils moved about in peace and quiet.

The sisters taught the children how to behave properly, and their manners improved day by day. Among the religious were many who had belonged to the aristocracy. These recalled their former ways of acting in the world and taught them to the children, who were insatiable in their desires. They learned how to behave like princes at their meals, and when they had to serve at table, they were like masters of the art. Though they had lost their natural appetites for food, they were delighted by the new knowledge they were acquiring and by the preciseness with which they were conducting their various activities. Gradually their appetites returned and their ability to fall easily asleep. The change wrought in these children made a profound impression. They could be seen running and jumping about, or carrying things in the garden, or bringing furniture out of the house and arranging it under the trees without breaking it or bumping into other objects. And all the while they showed their happiness in their cheerful faces.

It was then that the term "conversion" was first employed. "These children remind me of converts," observed one of the most famous Italian writers of the time. "There is no more miraculous conversion than one which conquers melancholy and depression and lifts one to a higher plane of life."

Despite its paradoxical expression, this concept made a deep impression on many minds. Conversion may seem to be contrary to the innocent state of childhood, and yet this term emphasized the spiritual character of the remarkable phenomenon that was apparent to all. The children had experienced a spiritual renewal which freed them from sorrow and abandonment and gave them a new birth of joy.

If we take sin and sadness as a kind of alienation from

a more perfect state, then the recovery of this state implies conversion. Sin and sadness then yield to joy.

The children were truly converted. They passed from a state of grief to happiness. They were freed from numerous, deep-seated defects. But there also was something more. Certain traits which are commonly esteemed also disappeared. In a dazzling fashion these children showed that men have erred and must be completely renewed. And this renewal is to be found in the springs of one's creative energies. If these poor children in our school, coming from almost hopeless conditions, had not shown this, it would have been impossible to distinguish what is truly good and evil in children since this had been determined beforehand in the minds of adults. The goodness of a child was measured by his adaptation to the conditions of adult life and vice versa. Because of this erroneous opinion the natural traits of children lay hidden. Adults no longer recognized what was good for, and in, the child as nature intended it to be.

21. PAMPERED CHILDREN

Another class of children living in unusual social conditions are the children of the wealthy. One might easily imagine that it would be much easier to educate them than the indigents of our first school or the orphans from Messina. But how are they to be "converted"? The children from wealthy families, surrounded as they are by all the luxuries that society can provide, seem to enjoy great privileges, but it will be sufficient to cite the experiences of teachers in Europe and America who have given me their first impressions and described the difficulties they encountered to counteract this opinion.

Children of this kind are not attracted by the paths of a garden, the beauty of flowers, and magnificent surroundings. They take no interest in objects which fascinate poorer children, and, as a consequence, their teacher becomes puzzled and disheartened since they will not pick out objects that should satisfy their own particular needs.

If children are poor, they will as a rule rush instantly toward the objects offered to them. But if they are rich and already satiated with elaborate toys, they rarely respond at once to the stimuli offered to them. An American teacher, Miss G., wrote to me as follows from Washington: "The children snatched the objects from each other's hands. If I tried to show something to one of them, the others would drop what they had in their hands and gather noisily about me. When I finished explaining an object, they would all fight for it. The children showed no real interest in the various materials. They passed from one object to another without lingering over any of them. One child was so incapable of staying in one place that he could not remain seated long enough to run his hands over any of the objects given to him. In many instances the movement of the children was aimless: they simply ran about the room heedless of the damage done. They ran into the table, upset chairs and trampled upon the material provided for them. Sometimes they would begin to work in one spot, then run off, take another object, and then abandon it for no reason whatever."

Mlle. D. wrote from Paris: "I must confess that my experiences were quite discouraging. The children could not concentrate on a task for more than a few minutes. They had no initiative, no perseverance. At times they followed each other about like a flock of sheep. When one child took an object the rest wanted to do the same. Sometimes they simply rolled on the floor knocking over the chairs."

The following laconic description comes from a school for rich children in Rome: "Our chief concern is discipline. The children are disoriented in work and refuse to take guidance."

But then there were turns for the better:

Miss G. continued with her experiences in Washington: "In a few days that nebulous mass of whirling particles (the disorderly children) began to take on a definite shape. It seemed as if the children began to give themselves direction. They started to take interest in objects which they had originally despised as silly toys. As a result of this new interest, they began to act as independent beings. An object which absorbed the complete attention of a child would not have the least attraction for another; the children pursued their own separate interests.

"The battle is finally won when a child finds something, some particular object, that spontaneously arouses his intense interest. Sometimes this enthusiasm comes suddenly and without warning. Once I attempted to stir up the interest of a child with nearly all the different objects used in the school without getting a single spark of attention. Then by chance I showed him two tablets, one red and the other blue, calling his attention to the different colors.

He immediately stretched out his hands as if he had been anxiously waiting for them and in a single lesson learned the five colors. During the following days he took up all the various objects that he had earlier scorned and gradually became interested in them all.

"One child, who at the beginning had a minimal span of attention, escaped from this state of chaos by becoming interested in one of the most complicated objects at his disposal, the so-called 'lengths.' He played continuously with these for a whole week and learned how to count and make simple additions. Then he began to return to simpler materials and became interested in all the various objects of the system.

"As soon as children find something that interests them they lose their instability and learn to concentrate."

This same teacher has given the following description of the awakening of a child's personality: "There were two sisters, one three and the other five years old. The three-year-old girl had no individuality of her own. She copied her older sister in everything. If the older girl had a blue pencil, the younger one was unhappy until she also had a blue pencil. If the elder ate bread and butter, the younger would eat nothing but bread and butter, and so on. The child had absolutely no interest in anything about the school: she simply followed her sister about, imitating her in everything she did. One day, however, she became interested in red cubes. She built a tower and repeated this exercise many times over, completely forgetting her sister. This puzzled the older girl so much that she called her and asked: 'Why are you building a tower when I am filling in a circle?' That day the little girl acquired a personality of her own and began to develop and ceased to be a simple reflection of her sister."

Mlle. D. gives an account of a four-year-old girl who was so utterly incapable of carrying a glass of water without spilling it, even when it was only half full, that she deliberately avoided the attempt. But then, after she had succeeded in another exercise in which she had become interested, she began to carry glasses of water without any difficulty and became engrossed in bringing water to her schoolmates who were painting with water colors, and she did this without spilling a drop.

Another very interesting fact has been reported to us by an Australian teacher. Miss B. had a little girl in school who could not speak but simply uttered indefinite sounds. Her parents were so concerned that they had taken her to a physician to see if she were retarded. One day this little girl got interested in the solid insets and spent a great deal of time in taking the wooden cylinders out of their holes and putting them back in. After she had done this over and over again with the keenest interest, she ran to the teacher saying, "Come and see!"

Mlle. D. further reports: "After the Christmas holidays, there was a great change in the class. It seemed that order was established by itself without any intervention on my part. The children seemed to be too occupied with their work to carry on aimlessly as they had done before. They went to the cabinet of their own accord to get the very objects which had formerly bored them. An atmosphere of work was created in the class. The children who had earlier chosen their objects at the promptings of a passing whim, now showed the need they had for a kind of inner discipline. They concentrated their efforts on exacting tasks and experienced a real satisfaction in overcoming difficulties. These precious efforts produced an immediate result upon their characters. They became their own masters."

An example which struck Mlle. D. was that of a four-and-a-half-year-old child with an extraordinarily developed imagination. This was so vivid that when an object was given to him he did not notice its shape but would immediately personify it and himself as well. He talked constantly and found it impossible to fix his attention on the object itself. Since his mind wandered so much, he was clumsy in his actions. He could not fasten even a single button. All at once something marvelous happened to him: "I was amazed at the change that came over him. He took up one exercise after the other and was thus able to calm himself."

These experiences of teachers who opened up schools before we had a fixed and definite method could be endlessly repeated, but they are much the same. Similar incidents and similar difficulties, though to a lesser degree, may be found in the lives of nearly all happy children who have intelligent and loving parents to watch over them. There are spiritual difficulties connected with material prosperity which explain why the words of Christ strike home in every heart: "Blessed are the poor in spirit! ... Blessed are they who mourn!"

But all are called and all, if they surmount their difficulties, can answer the call. The phenomenon of "conversion" thus belongs to childhood. It is a question of a rapid, and at times, almost instantaneous change that comes always from the same source. I would not be able to cite a single example of a conversion taking place without an interesting task that concentrated the child's activities. There are wide varieties of conversions that have occurred in this way. Children of a nervous temperament have become calm. The depressed have regained their spirits, and all have advanced together along the path of disciplined work, making progress through the outward manifestation of an inner energy which has found a means of expression.

These fixed attainments have an explosive character that foretells a child's later development. They may be compared to the sprouting of a child's first tooth or his first steps. The first tooth will be followed by others, the first word by speech, and after he has taken his first steps a child will begin to walk.

The diffusion of our schools throughout the world has shown the universality of these child conversions. Numerous childish traits fade away and are replaced by others. An initial error in the training of a child can be the source of countless deviations in his psychic life.

NORMALIZATION

What is to be particularly noted in these child conversions is a psychic cure, a return to what is normal. Actually the normal child is one who is precociously intelligent, who has learned to overcome himself and to live in peace, and who prefers a disciplined task to futile idleness. When we see a child in this light, we would more properly call his "conversion" a "normalization." Man's true nature lies hidden within himself. And this nature, which was given him at conception, must be recognized and allowed to grow.

But this interpretation does not remove the appearance of a child's conversion. Even an adult could perhaps be converted in the same way but the change would be so difficult that it could no longer be recognized as a simple return to the essentials of human nature.

In a child the normal psychic traits can flourish easily. Then all those traits that deviated from the norm disappear, just as with the return of health all the symptoms of a disease vanish.

If we would observe children in this light, we would ever more frequently recognize the spontaneous flowering of normality, even in the midst of a harsh environment. And though these indications of a normal development are rejected because they are not recognized or assisted, they still return as vital principles that thread their way through obstacles in their desire to succeed.

It might even be said that a child's normal energies, like the voice of Christ, teach us a lesson in forgiving, not seven times, "but seventy times seven." From the depths of his nature, the child repeatedly pardons the adult and strives to flourish despite the latter's repressions. He is engaged in a constant struggle against forces that would submerge his normal development.

22. THE SPIRITUAL PREPARATION OF THE TEACHER

A teacher, therefore, who would think that he could prepare himself for his mission through study alone would be mistaken. The first thing required of a teacher is that he be rightly disposed for his task.

The way in which we observe a child is extremely important. It is not sufficient to have a merely theoretical knowledge of education.

We insist on the fact that a teacher must prepare himself interiorly by systematically studying himself so that he can tear out his most deeply rooted defects, those in fact which impede his relations with children. In order to discover these subconscious failings, we have need of a special kind of instruction. We must see ourselves as another sees us.

This is equivalent to saying that a teacher must be initiated. He must begin by studying his own defects, his own evil tendencies, rather than by being excessively preoccupied with a "child's tendencies," with the manner of "correcting a child's mistakes," or even with "the effects of original sin." First remove the beam from your own eye and then you will see clearly how to remove the speck from the eye of a child.

This interior preparation of the teacher is something quite different from the "perfection" sought by a religion. A good teacher does not have to be entirely free from faults and weaknesses. In fact, one who is constantly seeking to perfect his own interior life may not notice the various defects that prevent him from understanding a child. We must be taught and we must be willing to accept guidance if we wish to become effective teachers.

Just as a doctor reveals to a patient the ills that afflict him, so we point out the defects in our future teachers that would hinder their work. We tell them, for example, "Anger is a great evil that can master us and keep us from understanding a child." And just as one sin never comes unaccompanied, so anger brings another evil—pride. It is concealed under the guise of good.

We can conquer our evil tendencies in two different ways, interiorly and exteriorly. The first way is by struggling against our known defects. The second way is by repressing the outward manifestations of our evil tendencies. External conformity to accepted standards of conduct is important since it makes us reflect and become aware of our faults. Respect for the opinion of one's neighbor enables one to conquer pride; straightened circumstances diminish avarice; a strong reaction on the part of another checks anger; a need to work in order to live conquers prejudices; social conventions are a check on loose conduct; difficulties in acquiring luxuries mitigate prodigality; and the need to retain one's dignity precludes envy. All of these various external factors can have a constant and salutary effect upon our inner life. Social relationships help to preserve our moral equilibrium.

Still we do not conform to social pressures with the same purity of intention that we obey God. If we readily enough admit the need of correcting errors which we recognize in ourselves, we do not so easily accept the humiliation of being corrected by others. We would rather make a mistake than admit it. When we have to amend our ways, we instinctively strive to save face and pretend that we have chosen what was inevitable. A proof of this may be seen in the little lie we tell when we say: "I didn't want it anyway," when we fail to obtain something which we desire. This is our instinctive reaction to external resistance. Instead of attempting to perfect ourselves interiorly, we continue the fight. And here, as in other battles, we soon find that our individual efforts have need of the help of others. Those who share the same defects instinctively assist each other, finding strength in their union.

We hide our defects under the guise of noble and impelling duties, just as in time of war offensive weapons are described as means for protecting peace. And the weaker the resistance is to our defects, the easier it is for us to organize our pretexts.

When we are criticized for our faults, we find it easy to excuse them. But in reality we are not defending ourselves but our mistakes, concealing them under the mask of what we call "beauty," "necessity," "the common good," and so forth. And little by little we convince ourselves of the truth of that which our conscience knows to be patently false and which becomes daily more difficult to correct.

Teachers, and in general all those concerned with the education of youth, should free themselves from this combination of errors that undermines their position. They should strive to rid themselves of their basic defect composed of pride and anger, seeing it in its true light. Anger is the principle defect, but it is cloaked by pride which lends it a certain dignity that can even demand respect.

But anger is an evil that is promptly resisted by our neighbors. Prudence demands that it be kept under control. And one who succeeds in thus humbling himself eventually comes to be ashamed of his temper.

When we are dealing with children, however, it is quite another story. They do not understand us, they cannot defend themselves from us, and they accept whatever we tell them. They not only accept abuse, but feel guilty whenever we blame them.

A teacher should reflect often upon a child's predicament. A child does not understand injustice with his reason, but he senses that something is wrong and becomes depressed and deformed. A child's unconscious reaction to the malice or thoughtlessness of adults finds expression in timidity, lying, errant behavior, crying without apparent reason, sleeplessness, and excessive fear, since he cannot grasp with his reason the cause of his depression.

In its primitive state anger implies a certain amount of physical violence, but it also finds expression in more subtle and refined ways which mask its real character. In its simplest form anger with a child is irritation at a child's resistance, but it soon becomes mingled with pride and develops into a kind of tyranny when confronted by the child's feeble attempts to express himself.

Tyranny defies discussion. It surrounds the individual with the impenetrable walls of recognized authority. Adults dominate children by virtue of a recognized natural right. To question this right would be the same as attacking a kind of consecrated sovereignty. If in a primitive community a tyrant represents God, an adult to a child is divinity itself. He is simply beyond discussion. Rather than disobey, a child must keep silent and adjust himself to everything.

If he does show some resistance, this will rarely be a direct, or even intended reply to an adult's action. It will rather be a vital defense of his own psychic integrity or an unconscious reaction to oppression.

Only with time does a child learn how to react directly against this tyranny. But by then an adult will have learned how to overcome a child by subtler means, convincing him that this tyranny is all for his own good.

A child owes respect to his elders, but adults claim the right to judge and even to offend a child. At their own convenience they direct or even suppress a child's needs, and his protests are regarded as a dangerous and intolerable lack of submission.

Adults here adopt the attitude of primitive rulers who exact tribute from their subjects without any right of appeal. Children who believe that they owe everything to adults are like those peoples who think that everything they possess is a gracious gift from their king. But are not adults responsible for this attitude? They have adopted the role of a creator and in their pride have maintained that they are responsible for everything that pertains to a child. They make him good, pious, and intelligent, and enable him to come into contact with his environment, with men, and with God. And to make the picture more complete, they refuse to admit that they are exercising any tyranny.

And yet has there ever been a tyrant who has ever admitted that he has preyed upon his subjects?

One who would become a teacher according to our system must examine himself and forgo this tyranny. He must rid his heart of pride and anger. He must learn how to humble himself and be clothed with charity. These are the virtues he must acquire, and this inner preparation will give him the balance and poise which he will need.

On the other hand, this does not mean that we must completely abstain from judging a child or that we must approve everything that he does or that we should neglect the development of his mind and feelings. Rather, a teacher should never forget that he is a teacher and that his mission is one of education.

But still we must be humble and root out the prejudices lurking in our hearts. We must not suppress those traits which can help us in our teaching, but we must check those inner attitudes characteristic of adults that can hinder our understanding of a child.

23. DEVIATIONS

Experience has shown that normalization causes the disappearance of many childish traits, not only those which are considered to be defects but also others which are generally thought to be virtues. Among the traits that disappear are not only untidiness, disobedience, sloth, greed, egoism, quarrelsomeness, and instability, but also the so-called "creative imagination," delight in stories, attachment to individuals, play, submissiveness, and so forth. They also include traits which have been scientifically studied and identified with childhood, such as imitation, curiosity, inconstancy, and wavering attention. The disappearance of these childish characteristics shows that the true nature of a child has hitherto not been understood. The universality of this fact is striking, but it is not entirely new since from earliest times a twofold nature has been recognized in man. The first was given to him at the time of his creation. The second came as a consequence of his first sin, a violation of God's law. Because of the fall man was deprived of the blessings of his earlier state and left to the mercy of his surroundings and the illusions of his own mind. This doctrine of original sin can help us understand what happens to a child.

A creature can be led astray by something that is in itself quite small. It is something that creeps in unnoticed under the guise of love and assistance but which is actually due to the blindness of an adult whose unconscious egoism can have a truly diabolical influence upon a child. And yet children are constantly being born anew, bearing within themselves unspoiled the plan according to which they should normally develop.

If a child's return to his normal, natural state is connected with a single specific factor, that is, his concentration upon some physical activity that puts him in contact
with exterior reality, we may conclude that there is a
single source for all his deviations—the child has not been
able to actualize his primitive plan of development because of the hostile environment he encountered in his
formative period when his potential energies should have
evolved through a process of *incarnation*.

FUGUES

The concept of incarnation can thus be taken as a guide
for interpreting deviant traits: psychic energy must be in-
carnated in movement so that it can unify the personality
of the agent. If this unity is not attained, either because of
adult domination or lack of motivation for the child in his
environment, the two constituent factors, psychic energy
and movement, develop separately and "the man is divided." Since nothing is created or destroyed in nature, a
child's psychic energies will either develop as they should
or go off in wrong directions. Such deviations generally
occur when these energies lose their finality and wander
aimlessly about. The mind, which should be building itself
up through voluntary, physical activites, then *takes refuge*
in fantasies.

When a fugitive mind fails to find something upon
which it may work, it becomes absorbed with images and
symbols. Children who are afflicted with this disorder
move restlessly about. They are lively, irrespressible, but
without purpose. They start something only to leave it
unfinished since their energies are directed toward many
different objects without being able to settle upon any of
them. Adults, even though they punish or patiently toler-
ate the errant and unruly actions of these disordered children, actually favor and encourage their fantasies, interpreting them as the creative tendencies of a child's mind.
Froebel invented many of his games to encourage the
development of a child's imagination along these lines. A

child is taught to see horses, castles, or trains in the bricks and blocks that he arranges in various ways. A child's imagination can give a symbolic meaning to any object whatever, but this creates fantastic mirages within his mind. A knob becomes a horse, a chair a throne, a stone an airplane. Children are given toys with which they can play, but which create illusions and afford no real and productive contact with reality. Toys furnish a child with an environment that has no particular goal and, as a consequence, they cannot provide it with any real mental concentration but only illusions. They can stir up a child's activity like a puff of air that rouses a tiny flame concealed beneath the ashes of a fire. But the flame is soon spent and the toy is soon thrown away. And yet toys are the only outlets that adults have found for a child's voluntary activity like a puff of air that rouses a tiny flame concealed their toys and believe that a child finds his happiness in them.

Even though a child easily tires of his toys and breaks them, this conviction persists; and adults are thought to be kind and generous when they lavish such gifts upon a child. Playing with toys is the only freedom that the world grants to a child, who should at this precious period by laying the foundations of a higher life. "Divided" children of this sort are regarded, particularly in school, as being highly intelligent, even if they lack order, neatness, and discipline.

In the surroundings which we provide for them we see these children immediately attach themselves to some task. Their excited fantasies and restless movements disappear and they calmly face reality and begin to perfect themselves through their work. They become normal children. Their aimless actions become directed. Their arms and legs become the instruments of minds eager to know and to penetrate the reality of their environment. A search for knowledge now replaces their aimless curiosity. With a brilliant insight, psychoanalysts have described the abnormal development of the imagination and excessive interest in play as a "psychic fugue."

A "fugue" is a kind of flight, a taking refuge. A flight into play or into a world of fancy often conceals an energy that has been divided. It represents a subconscious defense of the ego which flees from suffering or danger and hides itself behind a mask.

BARRIERS

Teachers discover that highly imaginative children are not the best in their studies as might be expected. Instead, they achieve little or nothing at all. Despite this fact no one suspects that the minds of these children have been diverted. Rather, it is thought that great creative intellects cannot apply themselves to practical matters. And yet the fact that a diverted child cannot control his thoughts or develop his mental powers as he should is an obvious indication that such a child is less intelligent. This weakening of a child's intellectual powers occurs not only when his mind takes flight into a world of illusions, but also when a child has become discouraged and seeks escape by withdrawing into himself. The average level of intelligence in ordinary children is low in comparison with that of normalized children. Because their energies have been misdirected, they are like children with broken bones who have need of special care if they are to become physically fit again. But instead of receiving the delicate treatment which they need for the correction of their psychic disorders and the furthering of their intellectual growth, children are frequently bullied about. A diverted mind cannot be forced and any such attempt to correct it in this way will provoke a psychological reaction.

This is not the commonly recognized psychological defense externally manifested in listlessness and disobedience. Rather it is a psychic defense completely outside the control of the will which unconsciously impedes the reception and understanding of ideas brought in from the outside.

It is a phenomenon described by psychoanalysts as "a psychic barrier." A teacher should be able to identify such a problem. A kind of veil descends upon a child's mind that renders it increasingly less responsive. Through this defensive mechanism the soul unconsciously says, "You speak, but I do not listen. You keep repeating, but I do not hear you. I cannot build up my own world since I am too busy erecting a wall to keep you out."

A prolonged defense of this kind causes a child to act as if he had lost the use of his natural faculties. There is no longer a question of good or bad will. In fact, teachers who are confronted with children afflicted with such psychic barriers believe that they are below average in intelligence and incapable of grasping certain types of material such as arithmetic and spelling.

If intelligent children erect psychic barriers against many different kinds of study and perhaps even against any kind of study whatever, they may be considered stupid; and if they repeat the same class several times over, they are considered to be mentally retarded. As a rule, a psychic barrier is not the only obstacle; it is surrounded by outer defenses known to psychoanalysts as "repugnances." There is first a repugnance for a particular subject, then for studies in general, then for the school, the teacher, and the child's companions. There is no longer room for love and cordiality, and the child finally fears school and becomes completely alienated from it.

Very frequently individuals carry with them through life a psychic barrier that was erected in childhood. An example of this may be found in the repugnance which many retain for mathematics as long as they live. They are not only unable to comprehend it, but the mere mention of it raises up an interior obstacle that worries and repels them. The same can also happen with other subjects. I once knew a young woman who was very intelligent, but who made truly inconceivable errors in spelling, considering her age and background. Every attempt to correct this defect proved to be useless. The errors seemed to multiply with practice. Even the reading of the classics proved ineffectual. But one day to my utter surprise, I saw her write beautifully and correctly. This is something which I cannot here take up in detail, but it is clear that she must have known the correct way to express herself. A secret force, however, held this ability in check, and all that appeared was a storm of errors.

CURES

The question might be raised as to which of the two modes of deviation, fugues or barriers, is the most serious. In our normalizing schools, fugues like those mentioned above connected with play or flights of fancy have proved to be the easier to cure. The reason for this may be seen in a comparison. If a person flees from a place, it is because he has not found in it what he needs; yet he can always return if there is a change in the environment from which he fled.

In fact, one of the things most frequently observed in our schools is the rapid transformation of disorderly and violent children. They seem to return almost instantly from a far-off land. There is not only a change in their disorderly habits of work, but a deeper change that is effected through the attainment of peace and satisfaction. The deviations disappear spontaneously. The child undergoes a natural transformation and yet, if he had not been freed from his deviations, these could have accompanied him throughout life. Many adults who seem to have a fertile imagination have in reality only vague feelings toward their surroundings and are dominated by their sense impressions. Such individuals are known for their imaginative temperament. They are without order, but are ready admirers of lights, of the sky, of colors, flowers, landscapes, of music, and they have a sentimental and romantic outlook on life.

But they do not know the light which they admire well enough to really love it. The stars that inspire them cannot hold their attention long enough for them to attain the least knowledge of astronomy. They have artistic tendencies but they produce nothing since they lack the perseverance to acquire any technical skill. As a rule, they do not know what to do with their hands. They cannot keep them quiet, nor can they put them to work. They touch things nervously and frequently break them. They absentmindedly pluck up the flowers that they admire. They cannot create anything beautiful nor make their own lives happy. They do not know how to discover the poetry that is to be found in the world. They are lost if no one assists them since they take their failures and their organic weaknesses as marks of perfection. These defects, which can develop into serious psychic maladies, had their origins in their early years when one is most easily confused and when a barred road causes deviations which are imperceptible at the beginning.

Barriers, on the other hand, are quite difficult to overcome, even when they are found in little children. An inner wall is built up which closes the spirit and conceals it as a defense against the world. Behind these multiple barriers a hidden drama is unfolded, since the soul is frequently separated from all that is beautiful outside that could be a source of happiness. The pursuit of knowledge, the secrets of science and mathematics, the fascinating charm of music are all "enemies" of a man who isolates himself. His natural energies are perverted so that they darken and conceal everything that would be an object of interest and love. Studies lead to weariness and a repugnance for the world instead of preparing a child to take a place in it.

"Barriers" is a highly suggestive word. It makes us think of the means used to ward off diseases before there was any true knowledge of hygiene. Men and women avoided contact with fresh air, water, and the sun. They remained shut up behind walls that were impermeable to light. They kept their windows closed by day and night, even though these were already too small for proper ventilation. They wrapped themselves up in heavy garments, one on top of the other like the layers of an onion, thus preventing the air from cleansing the pores of their skin. Their physical environment was a veritable barricade against life itself.

But there are aspects of society that also make us think of barriers. Why do men isolate themselves from each other, and why does each family group shut itself off with a feeling of aloofness and repugnance towards other groups? A family does not seek to be alone so that it can find its pleasures within its own circle, but to separate itself from others. Walls are not built to protect love. A family's defenses are closed, insurmountable, stronger than the walls of the house in which it dwells and, as a consequence, are the real barriers which separate men into social castes and nations.

National barriers were not erected to separate one united, homogenous group from another and furnish it with freedom and protection. Rather, this longing for isolation and defense strengthens the barriers already existing between nation and nation and hinders the exchange of persons and commodities.

But if civilizations develop through a mutual exchange of materials and ideas, what lies behind this lack of trust? Can it be perhaps that even nations suffer from these psychic barriers that are the products of suffering and violence? Pain and sorrow have become organized and the suffering has been so intense that the life of nations has drawn back behind barriers that are ever more terrible and entrenched.

ATTACHMENT

Some children are of such a retiring nature that their psychic energies are too weak to resist the influence of an adult. Instead, they attach themselves to an older person who tends to substitute his own activity for theirs and they thus become extremely dependent upon him. Their lack of vital energy, although they are not aware of it themselves, makes them prone to tears. They complain about everything; and since they have the air of one who is suffering, they are thought to be sensitive and affectionate. They are always bored, though they do not realize it, and they have recourse to others, that is, to adults, because they cannot

by themselves escape the boredom that oppresses them.
They cling to another as if their very life depended upon
it. They ask an adult for help. They want him to play with
them, to tell them stories, to sing to them, and never to
leave them. An adult becomes a slave to such children.
Even though child and adult seem to have a deep understanding and affection for one another, they are ensnared
in the same net. Children such as these are constantly
asking "why" something is so, as if they were eager for
knowledge. But if we observe them closely, we notice that
they do not listen to the answers given them, but simply
keep repeating their questions. What seems to be an eager
curiosity is in reality a means of keeping a person whom
they need for support near at hand.

They readily give up their own activities and obey the
least bidding of an adult, who finds it easy to substitute his
own will for that of a docile child. But there is a grave
danger that this will cause a child to lapse into a kind of
apathy that can be taken as sloth or laziness.

An adult is pleased with such a state of affairs since the
child is no hindrance to his own activities. But this only
emphasizes the serious character of this deviation.

Indolence is in reality a spritual sickness. It may be
compared to the weakness of a person who is seriously ill.
It is the external manifestation of a decline of vital,
creative energies. Christianity recognizes sloth as one of
the capital sins, as one of the evils that can bring death to
the soul.

Without realizing it, an adult with his useless assistance
and hypnotic influence has substituted himself for a child
and impeded his psychic growth.

POSSESSIVENESS

In tiny infants and in normalized children there is a
natural tendency to make use of their various faculties.
They are not indifferent to their environment, but are
deeply in love with it. They are like hungry individuals
in search of food. This longing for something to satisfy a

physical need is not the product of reasoning. We do not say, for example: "It is a long time since I have eaten; if I do not eat, I will not be able to retain my strength or even stay alive. I must therefore look for something nourishing to eat." No, hunger is rather a kind of pain that irresistibly drives us on in a search of food. A child has a comparable hunger for his environment. He seeks for things that can nourish his spirit, and he finds his nourishment in activity.

As newborn children "let us love spiritual milk." This drive, this love for his environment is innate in man. It would not be right to say that a child is passionately in love with his environment, since passion is something that is impulsive and transitory. Rather it should be described as an impulse towards "a vital experience." The drive behind the child's love for his environment urges him on to ceaseless activity. The fire that burns him could be compared with the heat that is generated in the body by the oxygen of the air. An active child creates the impression of one living in a suitable environment, that is, in an environment that contributes to his self-realization. If a child does not have such an environment his psychic life is not developed but remains weak, warped, and apart from the world. The child himself becomes an enigma. He is helpless, without resources, bored, subject to whims, and unsociable.

If a child finds no stimuli for the activities which would contribute to his development, he is attracted simply to "things" and desires to possess them. To take something and keep it is easy and requires little knowledge and love. A child's energies are thus diverted. Such a child will say, "I want it," when he sees a gold watch, even though he cannot tell time. But then another child will immediately shout, "No, I want it," and they are ready to fight over the watch even if this might ruin it. This is the way in which individuals begin to compete against each other and destroy the objects they desire to possess.

Practically all moral deviations flow from this first step that makes a decision between love and possession. One who has made such a choice advances along one of two diverging roads. A child's natural energies reach out like the tentacles of an octopus to seize and destroy the objects that he passionately desires. A feeling of ownership makes him cling tenaciously to things, and he defends them as he would defend his own life. Strong and active children defend their possessions by fighting off other children who would like to have them. Children of this sort, since they want the same objects, are constantly quarreling among themselves. This gives rise to painful reactions—harsh feelings and quarrels over trivialities. Such disputes should not be taken lightly. There is something out of joint, and darkness where there should be light. And this has happened because one's natural energies have been diverted. Possessiveness has its origin in some inner evil and not in an external object.

As part of their moral training, children are urged not to attach themselves to material things. The basis of this instruction is respect for the property of others. But when a child has arrived at this point, it has already crossed the bridge which separates one from a deep interior life, and this is why he eagerly turns to external things. A child is so penetrated with this desire that it is thought to be a part of his very nature.

Children of a retiring temperament also turn their attention to worthless, material objects. These children, however, possess things in a different way. They are not contentious and usually do not compete with others. They rather tend to accumulate and conceal things. They are thought to be collectors, but they do not collect objects in order to classify them into rational categories. They accumulate objects that are highly diversified and have nothing to do with each other. Not only mentally sick adults, but delinquent children as well, who frequently have their pockets filled with useless and ill-sorted objects, have an irrational mania for collecting. Children of a weak and retiring character engage in similar activities, but their habits of accumulating things are regarded as perfectly normal. If anyone attempts to deprive these children of the objects they have collected, they put themselves on their guard to the best of their ability.

The psychologist Adler has given an interesting interpretation to this habit of collecting. He compares it with the avarice of adults, the germs of which can be already recognized in infancy. A man's attachment to many things and his reluctance to give them up even if they are of no use to him is a deadly poison that can upset his basic equilibrium. Parents are pleased at seeing their children defend their property. They look on this as a part of human nature and as an important factor in society. Children who are possessive and collectors are types recognized and understood by the average man.

DESIRE FOR POWER

Another deviant characteristic associated with possessiveness is a desire for power. One kind of power may be recognized in the instinct to dominate one's environment and thus gain possession of the outer world through a love of this environment. But this power becomes diverted when, instead of being the natural outcome of psychic growth, it is reduced to mere covetousness.

A deviated child finds himself in the presence of an adult who, as far as he is concerned, is a supremely powerful being with everything at his disposal. Such a child realizes that his own power will be great if he can act through an adult. He begins to exploit the adult so that he can obtain far more than he ever could through his own unaided efforts. This is a perfectly understandable procedure, and one that little by little so infects all children that it is thought to be something very ordinary, though difficult to correct. In reality it is a classic trick on the part of a child. There is nothing more natural and reasonable than that a weak and helpless child, once he has discovered that he can make use of another powerful individual, should start to do so. He begins to make demands beyond what an adult thinks to be right. His desires, in fact, are limitless. To an imaginative child an adult is omnipotent and capable of fulfilling his most extravagant and fickle wishes. Such an attitude finds its full realization in the fairy tales that are so appealing to a child's soul. A child feels his obscure desires delightfully portrayed in these fantastic stories. One who has resource to fairies can obtain riches and favors far beyond mere human powers. There are good fairies and bad fairies, beautiful fairies and ugly fairies. They are found among the poor as well as among the rich, in woods as well as in enchanting palaces. They are the projection of the imagination of a child who lives among adults. There are old fairies like his grandmother and young, beautiful fairies like his mother. Some of these fairies are dressed in rags and others are clothed in silk and gold, just as there are poor mothers and rich mothers with their fine clothes, but they all spoil their children.

An adult, however high or low he may be, is always a powerful being in comparison with a child. Carried away by his dreams, a child begins to exploit him. At first the adult is pleased and delights in seeing the happiness he gives his child. But his concessions lead to grief. An adult will help his child to wash his hands, but he will later pay for yielding to this demand. After an initial victory, a child looks for a second, and the more an adult yields the more the child craves. Eventually the illusion that an adult was made to satisfy a child's desires is dissolved into bitterness. Since the material world is severely limited, whereas the imagination can wander out into infinity, there comes at last a clash and violent struggle. A child's whims become the scourge of an adult who suddenly realizes that he has been at fault and says: "I have spoiled my child."

Even a submissive child has his own way of conquering. He gains his victories through affection, through tears, entreaties, a melancholy look, and even through his natural charm. An adult may yield to such a child until he can give no more, and then a state of bitterness is reached which leads to all kinds of deviations. The adult comes to his senses and realizes that his own way of acting has been the source of his child's defects, and he looks around for a means of correcting them.

But we know that nothing can correct a child's whims. Neither exhortation nor punishment are efficacious. It is like telling one delirious with a fever that he should get well and threatening to beat him if his temperature does not go down. No, an adult did not spoil his child when he yielded to him, but when he hindered his growth and caused his natural development to go astray.

THE INFERIORITY COMPLEX

Adults manifest a contempt for children which they fail to realize. Though a father may believe that his child is beautiful and perfect, and though he may center in him his pride and hopes for the future, a secret urge makes him act as if he were convinced that his child was "empty" and "bad" and thus in need of filling and correction. This obscure attitude constitutes the adult's contempt for a child. He looks upon the weak child before him as his own and to be treated as he pleases. He sees nothing wrong in revealing to a child traits of character that he would be ashamed to manifest in the company of adults. Within the domestic walls his greed and tyranny, disguised as paternal authority, are constantly breaking down the child's ego. If, for example, an adult sees a child carrying a glass of water, he begins to fear that the glass may be broken, and when he feels this way, his greed makes him regard the glass as a treasure and he takes it from the child. The adult who does this may even be very wealthy and intent upon increasing his fortunes many times over in order to make his son still more wealthy than himself. But for the moment he esteems a glass as something of greater value than his child's activity and seeks to prevent its being broken. He thinks within himself, "Why does this child have to set a glass down in this way when I do it in another? Can't I arrange things as I please?" And yet this same adult would gladly make any sacrifice for his child. He dreams of the child's success. He would like to see him become a famous and powerful man. But at this moment he is swayed by an authoritarian, tyrannical impulse that wastes his energies protecting a worthless object. In fact, if a servant were to handle the glass in the same way as the child, the father would simply smile; and if a guest were to break the glass he would immediately be reassured that the glass was worthless and the accident of no account.

A child, therefore, must notice with a continued sense of frustration that he is the only one thought to be unreliable and a source of harm. He thus comes to look upon himself as an inferior being, worth less than the objects he is forbidden to touch.

Some other facts must also be taken into account. If a child is to develop his interior life, he must not only be allowed to touch various objects and work with them but he must do this in a rational and consistent fashion. All of this is of the utmost importance for the development of his personality. An adult no longer pays any deliberate attention to the succession of ordinary acts in daily life since they have become a part of his pattern of existence. When an adult rises in the morning, he knows by habit what he must do and carries out his ordinary actions as if they were the simplest things in the world. The sequence of his acts is almost automatic and no more noticed than the air he breathes or the beating of his heart.

A child, on the other hand, has yet to develop his habits of acting, but he is never allowed to lay out a continuous course of action. If a child is playing, an adult interrupts him, thinking that it is time for a walk. The child is dressed and taken out. Or a child may be working at a task such as filling a pail with stones when a friend of his mother calls. The child is then interrupted in his work and shown to the visitor. An adult is constantly interrupting the child and breaking into his environment. This powerful being directs the child's life without ever consulting the child himself. And this lack of consideration makes the child think that his own activities are of no value. On the other hand, when an adult addresses another adult in a child's presence even though this may be a servant, he does not interrupt him without saying, "If you please," or "if you can." A child consequently feels that he is different from the rest of mankind, that he is inferior, subject to all.

As we have already noted, a succession of acts dependent upon an interiorly preconceived plan is of utmost importance for a child's development. One day an adult will explain to a child that he is responsible for his own actions. Such a responsibility is dependent upon a thorough understanding of the connection between his various actions and a normal judgment with regard to their meaning, but a child only feels that his every action is insignificant. A father who is grieved that he has not succeeded in arousing a sense of responsibility and self-control in his son is the very one who has destroyed his child's sense of continuity in his actions and his regard for his own dignity. The child bears within himself a secret conviction of inferiority and impotence. And yet, before anyone can assume a responsibility, he must be convinced that he is the master of his own actions and have confidence in himself.

The greatest source of discouragement is the conviction that one is unable to do something. If one who is paralyzed had to race with another who is perfectly sound, he would not wish to race at all. An ordinary citizen would not care to meet a professional boxer in the ring. A feeling of incompetence discourages effort even before one is put to the test. An adult, by constantly humiliating a child and making him aware of his weaknesses, dampens the child's desire to act. But an adult is not content with simply impeding a child's activities; he keeps telling him, "You can't do that; it is useless for you even to try." If the adult is rude he will even say, "You idiot, what are you doing? Don't you know you can't do that?" But such a manner of acting not only impedes a child at his work and interrupts the continuity of his actions, but it is an insult to the child himself.

This leads the child to believe that not only are his actions worthless but that he is personally helpless and inept. This conviction in turn is a source of discouragement and diffidence. If one stronger than ourselves prevents us from doing what we want, we can at least conjecture that there will be another weaker than we are who will not prevent us from doing what we would like in the future. But if an adult persuades a child that his impotency lies within himself, a cloud descends upon his mind and he sinks into a state of apathy and fear. When this happens, a child develops that inner obstacle known as an "inferiority complex." Such an obstacle can become fixed within him as a feeling of impotency and inferiority with respect to others; and it keeps the child from becoming engaged in the conflicts of daily existence.

Timidity, hesitancy in the making of decisions, a withdrawal before difficulties or criticism, frequent tears, and an appearance of despair accompany the painful state created by an inferiority complex.

On the other hand, one of the most remarkable characteristics of a "normal" child is his self-confidence and sureness in action.

When the little boy at San Lorenzo told the disappointed visitors that the children could open up the classroom and set to work even though the teacher was absent because it was a holiday, he showed the balance of a well-rounded personality that is not presumptuous but still knows its potentialities. The boy knew what he was doing and brought the necessary sequence of acts to completion without feeling that he had done anything exceptional.

Another little boy who was using movable letters to put words together was not at all disturbed when the queen of Italy stopped in front of him and asked him to spell out *"Viva l'Italia!"* When the child heard this, he put the letters which he had been using back in their proper order. He did this as calmly as if he had been alone, though one might have expected him to suspend this work in honor of the queen so that he could carry out her bidding at once. But he could not give up his habitual manner of working. Before he could compose new words, he had to put the letters already used back in their proper places. When he had done this, he then spelled out the words, *"Viva l'Italia!"* Though this little fellow was only four years old, he was in reality already a little man in control of his actions and emotions and secure in his environment.

FEAR

Fear is another form of deviation which is thought to be natural in children. It is understood as an emotional disturbance deeply rooted within a child and quite independent of his surroundings. In other words, fear, like shyness, is taken as a part of a child's character. Some children are so retiring they seem to be enveloped in an aura of fear. There are others, however, who are brave, active, and often courageous in the face of danger, but who can at times be subject to mysterious, illogical, and invincible alarms. Such attitudes may be explained as the products of vivid impressions received in the past. Children may be afraid to cross a street, or that there are cats under a bed, or they may fear the sight of a hen. These fears are like the phobias noted by psychiatrists in adults. They are found especially in children who are dependent upon adults. And an adult can take advantage of a child's ignorance to frighten him with vague fears so that he will be obedient. This is one of the worst defenses that an adult employs against a child since it aggravates the child's natural fear of the dark by peopling it with frightful images.

Anything that enables a child to come into contact with reality and to experience and understand his environment will help to free him from this disturbing state of fear. One of the first fruits of our normalizing schools is the disappearance of these subconscious fears.

A Spanish family had four girls, the youngest of whom attended one of our schools. Whenever there was a storm during the night, she was the only one of the girls who did not become afraid. She would bring her older sisters to their parent's room, where they could find protection. She was a true support to her older sisters afflicted with this strange fear. Whenever they became frightened in the dark, they would hasten to their little sister to overcome their anxiety.

A "state of fear" is different from that dread aroused by the instinct of self-preservation in the face of danger. This latter type of fear is less frequent in children than in adults, and not simply because children are less experienced than their elders in meeting dangers. It might even be said that a child naturally confronts dangers and does so with greater readiness than adults. As a matter of fact, children often expose themselves to peril. Street urchins steal rides on moving cars or trucks, and in the country children climb high up in the trees and slide down steep slopes. They plunge into the sea or a river and often teach themselves how to swim. In countless cases they have shown great heroism in saving, or at least attempting to save, their companions. For example, a fire broke out in a hospital in California which contained a ward for blind children. Among the victims were several children who could see. Although they lived in another part of the building, they had rushed to assist the blind. And almost every day we read in newspapers or magazines of other examples of youthful heroism.

The question might be raised as to whether or not a child's return to a normal state favors this heroic tendency. None of the children in our schools have performed any heroic feats, though they have on occasion expressed some truly noble desires. As a rule our children develop a kind of "prudence," which enables them to avoid dangers and consequently to live with them. They can handle knives at a table and even in the kitchen, use matches for lighting a fire or even sparklers, stand alone near pools of water, and cross city streets. Our children have learned how to control their actions and to avoid rashness. This enables them to lead a nobler and more peaceful life. Normalization, therefore, does not consist in hurling oneself into the midst of dangers, but in acquiring a prudence which permits one to recognize and dominate dangers and thus be in a position to live in the midst of them.

LIES

Psychic deviations can shoot out in all directions like the branches of a luxuriant plant, but they all spring from the same deep roots, and it is only there that the secret of normalization is to be found. A common mistake of educators is to consider these deviations as separate entities independent of each other.

One of the most serious defects is lying. Deceit is a kind of garment that conceals the soul. It might even be compared to a whole wardrobe, so many are its guises. There are many different kinds of lies, each having its own meaning and significance. There are normal lies and others that are pathological. Psychiatrists of the last century were much interested in the compulsive lies of men and women subject to hysteria. In such individuals lying grows to such a proportion that speech becomes a whole tissue of deceit. Attention has also been drawn to the lies of children in juvenile courts, and to the possibility of unconscious deceit on the part of children summoned as witnesses. A considerable stir was created when men came to realize that a child, whose "innocent soul" is looked upon as the mouthpiece of truth, could in all sincerity state that something was true which was actually false. Further study of this phenomenon showed that these children were actually trying to tell the truth and that their lying was due to a mental confusion that had been exaggerated by their emotions.

Such substitutions of falsehood for truth, whether they be chronic or isolated, are quite distinct from the lies which a child deliberately imploys as a defense behind which he can hide. But there are still other lies which are not connected with self-defense, and they are told by normal children in the ordinary circumstances of life. Lying can also have its origin in a child's desire to narrate something fantastic, and an invention of this sort can have the added relish of being taken by others as the truth, even though it is not recounted for the sake of deceit or personal gain. It can take on an artistic form like that of an actor who identifies himself with his role. A number of children, for example, once told me that their mother had given a person whom she had invited in for dinner some vegetable juices that she had prepared herself. The drink was not only healthful but so delicious that the guest said he had never tasted anything like it before. The story was so interesting and detailed that I asked the children's mother to tell me how to prepare the drink. But she then told me that she had never made anything of the kind. Here we have an instance of a pure creation in a child's imagination expressed in a lie with no other intent than that of concocting a story.

These lies are different from the kind told because a child is lazy and is not interested in discovering the truth.

Sometimes, however, a lie can be the product of subtle reasoning. I once knew a five-year-old boy who had been temporarily left by his mother in a boarding school. The governess in charge of the group of children to which he belonged was admirably suited for the task and had a high regard for this particular child. After a time he began to complain to his mother about her, saying that she was entirely too severe. His mother went to the principal of the school to make inquiries and became convinced of the affection which the governess had for her son and which she had constantly shown him. When the woman asked her son why he had lied, he replied, "I couldn't say that the principal was bad." It does not seem that he lacked courage to accuse the principal but rather that he was subject to the force of convention. Much more could be said of the cunning used by children in adapting themselves to their environment.

Weak and retiring children, in turn, make up lies on the spur of the moment. Such lies are not carefully thought out, but are rather a kind of defensive reflex. They are naive, improvised, and consequently quite obvious. Teachers combat deceit of this sort, but forget what they represent. They are an obvious defense against the assaults of adults. Children who are guilty of such lies are accused of being weak, shameless, and failing to act as they should.

Deceit is an intellectual phenomenon that appears in childhood, but which becomes organized with maturity. It plays such an important role in human society that it seems to be indispensable, noble, and even beautiful, like clothes for the body. A child in one of our schools gives up this perverted notion and appears natural and sincere. Nevertheless, lying is not a deviation that disappears miraculously. There is more need of reconstruction than conversion. Clear ideas, a contact with reality, freedom of spirit, and an active interest in what is good and noble provide the environment that can straighten out a child's soul.

Social life is so immersed in an atmosphere of false conventions that society would be thrown into a turmoil if an attempt were made to correct them. Many children who have left the Children's Homes for more advanced schools have been thought to be impertinent and disobedient simply because they were much more sincere than other children and had not learned to make the necessary adaptations. Their teachers did not recognize this fact. The discipline and conventions of an ordinary school, like those of society, are shot through with deceit, and these teachers took the hitherto unknown sincerity of the children from our schools as a factor that would disrupt the education of others.

One of the most brilliant contributions of psychoanalysis to the history of the human soul has been the interpretation of the subconscious camouflages. Adult shame and not childish fictions, make up the terrible fabric of human life. They are like the fur of an animal or the feathers of a bird that cover, adorn, and protect the vital principle that lies hidden beneath. Camouflage, the concealing of one's true feelings, is the lie that a man builds up within himself so that he can live, or rather, survive in a world at odds with his natural sentiments. And since it is impossible to be engaged in a constant struggle, the soul adapts itself to its surroundings.

One of the most remarkable camouflages is the hypocrisy with which an adult treats a child. An adult sacrifices a child's needs to his own, but he refuses to recognize the fact, since this would be intolerable. He persuades himself that he is exercising a natural right and acting for the future good of the child. When the child defends himself, the adult does not advert to what is really happening but judges whatever the child does to save himself as disobedience and the result of his evil tendencies. The feeble voice of truth and justice within the adult grows weak and is replaced by the false conviction that one is acting prudently, according to one's right and duty, and so forth. The heart is hardened. It becomes like ice and gleams like crystal. Everything is broken against it. "My heart has become a rock; I strike it and my hand is injured." Dante uses the magnificent image of ice in the abyss of hell where hate finds its refuge. Love and hate are two states of the soul which can be compared to water in its liquid and solid states. Conventions which camouflage a man's true feelings are a spiritual lie which help him adapt himself to the organized deviations of society but which gradually change love into hatred. This is the terrible lie lurking in the deepest recesses of the subconscious.

24. REPERCUSSIONS ON PHYSICAL HEALTH

Psychic deviations bring a wide variety of traits along with them. Some of these may seem to be unrelated since they affect the functioning of the body. Modern medicine has thoroughly studied and established the fact that many physical disturbances have a psychic origin. Even certain defects which seem to be intimately connected with the body have their ultimate source in psychic problems. Some of these, such as difficulties with digestion, are particularly common among children. Strong and active children tend to have a voracious hunger which is hard to control. These children eat more than is necessary. Their insatiable desire for food is often lightly taken as "a good appetite," even though they may become sick and need medical assistance.

From antiquity a craving for more food than the body needs, which results in more harm than good, has been recognized as a vice. In this craving may be seen the degeneration of a normal sensibility which prompts one to eat, but which also determines the amount of food required. Such a sensibility is characteristic of all animals whose well-being is determined by their instinct for self-preservation. And, as a matter of fact, this instinct has a twofold aspect. One of these concerns the animal's environment and guides it in the avoidance of dangers. The other is proper to the individual itself and has reference to the taking of food. Brute animals have a guiding instinct which not only induces them to eat what they should, but also in the measure that is good for them. Indeed, this is one of the most distinctive characteristics of every species of animal. Whether they eat much or only a little, every animal eats the amount of food that its instinct tells it to take.

Only man is guilty of the vice of gluttony, which blindly leads him to eat not only more than he should but also what is actually harmful. We can therefore say that with the appearance of psychic deviations individuals lose the sensibilities which would protect them and assure their state of health. Proof of this may be found in a deviated child, who soon begins to show a lack of balance in his eating habits. The child is attracted by the sight of food, which is judged only by the external sense of taste. The instinct of self-preservation, the vital interior force is weakened and disappears. One of the most striking things about our normalizing schools is the fact that children who have been freed from their psychic deviations and have acquired a normal state lose their greedy craving for food. They become interested in eating correctly and with the proper gestures. When the time came to eat, tiny children would occupy their time with properly arranging their napkins, with looking at their knives, forks, and spoons in an effort to remember the exact way to hold and use them, or in assisting a companion smaller than themselves. And sometimes they were so meticulous about these matters that the tasty food set before them grew cold. Other children appeared sad: they had hoped to be chosen to serve at table, but saw themselves instead condemned to an easier task, that of eating.

A further proof of the relation between food and a person's psychological state may be seen in the attitude of retiring children. Such children have a notable, and often unconquerable, repugnance for food. Many refuse to take anything to eat and at times their refusal can be so emphatic that it creates real difficulties within a family or boarding school. This is particularly striking in institutions for poor, weak children, who might be expected to eat their fill whenever they could. At times a lack of interest in food can bring a child to such a physical state that he resists all cure. But this repugnance for eating should not be confused with a physical disorder that causes a child to lose his appetite. Rather, the child refuses to eat because of his psychic condition. In some cases, this may be due to a defense mechanism. An adult, for example, tries to make the child eat in a hurry, but a child has his own particular rhythm for eating and refuses to accept that of the adult. This is a fact now recognized by pediatricians who note that children do not eat all they need at once, but stop eating for considerable periods of time.

The same may also be noticed in infants before they are weaned. They withdraw from their source of nourishment before they are full in order to rest, and then return to it in a kind of slow, intermittent rhythm. When a child refuses to eat, a possible reason for this may thus be found in a barrier which a child has erected against those who would force him to eat in a way opposed to his own natural tendencies. There are instances, however, where this particular type of defense must be ruled out and the source of the trouble must be sought elsewhere. The child seems almost to be constitutionally lacking in appetite. He is hopelessly pale and no exposure to the open air, the sun, or the sea can conquer his habitual repugnance for food. On closer examination, however, we will find that there is near the child an adult to whom he is extremely attached, but who completely dominates him. There is only one way to cure such a child, and that is to remove the person who represses him and provide an environment where he will be psychologically free and active. Only in this way will he rid himself of the attachment that has deformed his spirit.

The connection between one's psychic life and physical phenomena that seem to be far from it, such as the taking of food, has always been recognized. In the Old Testament we read how Esau, because of his gluttony, yielded his birthright to his brother, foolishly acting against his own best interests. Indeed, gluttony is listed among the vices that "obscure the mind." It is interesting to see the precision with which St. Thomas Aquinas points out the ties between gluttony and the intellect. He maintains that gluttony dulls one's judgment and as a consequence weakens one's knowledge of intelligible realities. But the very opposite of this is found in a child: it is the psychic disturbance that engenders gluttony.

Christianity has so closely connected this vice with spiritual disorders that it places it among the capital sins, that is, among those that lead to the death of the soul; in other words, it leads to a violation of one of the mysterious laws of the universe. Further support for our theory of the blunting of the guiding instinct, that is, of the tendency for self-preservation, has been indirectly given by psychoanalysis. But this modern science interprets it in a different fashion and speaks of a "death instinct." It recognizes in man a natural tendency to assist and facilitate the natural advent of death and to hasten its coming even to the point of committing suicide. A man can become hopelessly attached to such poisons as alcohol, opium, and cocaine. Instead of clinging to life and salvation, he becomes enamored with death and calls it to himself. But does not all this indicate in a very precise fashion the disappearance of a vital interior sensibility which ought to watch over the preservation of the individual? If such a tendency were connected with the inevitability of death, it should be found in all creatures. But since it is not, we must say that every psychic deviation sets a man on the road to death and leads him on to destruction, and that this terrible tendency may already be seen in an almost imperceptible form in early childhood.

Illnesses may always have something psychological about them, since man's physical and psychic lives are so intimately connected. But abnormalities in the taking of food open up the gates to all kinds of sicknesses. Sometimes a person may only be apparently sick. It is in reality only an imaginary illness and its source is psychological. A great contribution to our understanding of these abnormalities was made by psychoanalysis which showed that a person can find a kind of refuge in sickness. Such escapes are not simply feigned. There can be rises in temperature and functional disorders that at times seem serious. And yet there is no real sickness. The symptoms are due to subconscious psychic disorders which succeed in dominating the laws of physiology. Through this type of illness the ego can withdraw from unpleasant situations or obligations. The disease resists all treatment and only disappears when the ego is freed from the conditions it sought to escape. Many illnesses and morbid states, like many moral defects, disappear when children are placed in a free environment where they can live and act in a way that brings them back to normal. Today many pediatricians recognize our schools as Health Homes (*Case della Salute*). They send children with functional illnesses that have resisted ordinary treatment to them, and astonishing cures have thus been obtained.

PART III

25. THE CONFLICT BETWEEN ADULT AND CHILD

The conflict between adult and child has consequences reaching out almost to infinity, like the waves that are propagated when a stone is thrown into the surface of a tranquil lake. A disturbance is started that spreads out in a circle in all directions.

Just as an examination of the ripples of the water will lead one back to the cause of the disturbance, so psychoanalysts and physicians have been able to trace physical and mental diseases back to their origins. But they must travel long distances in their search for the sources of mental ills. They are like the first explorers of the Nile who had to travel thousands of miles and negotiate fantastic cataracts before they reached the calm waters of the great lakes that feed the river. Sciences that seek to probe the causes of the weaknesses and failures of the human soul must go beyond immediate causes and, passing beyond what is consciously known, arrive at the original sources, the peaceful lakes, that are the body and soul of the child. But if we wish to travel in an opposite direction, if we are interested in the history of humanity as it has been newly written from its primitive beginnings, we can start from the limpid lakes of early childhood and follow life's dramatic course as it frees itself and rushes rapidly along, leaping from one cataract to another, completely free except for one thing, that is, to stop, to cease to augment its tumultuous waters.

If the physical, mental, and nervous diseases that afflict adults can be traced to childhood, it is in the life of a child that we can notice their first symptoms. Moreover, it will be well to keep in mind that every great and obvious evil is accompanied by an infinity of lesser ills. More people are cured of a disease than die from it. And if sickness represents a breakdown in one's ability to resist the onslaught of a disease, other failures of the same type may be anticipated.

There are countless things that can occasion the collapse of one's physical or mental health. When water is examined to see if it is fit to drink, only a small sample needs to be drawn. If this is tainted, we may conclude that the rest is tainted as well. Somewhat similarly, when we see numerous individuals perishing through their own mistakes, we may conclude that the whole human race has been afflicted by some basic error.

This is not a new concept. Already in the time of Moses it was known that the first man sinned and that his sin brought ruin on all mankind. To those who do not understand its true nature, original sin may seem to be unjust and unreasonable since it involves the condemnation of all of Adam's descendants. And yet we see under our very eyes innocent children condemned to carry within themselves the fatal consequences of centuries of error with respect to their natural development. The sources of these errors are to be found in the basic conflicts of human life, and they are freighted with consequences that have not as yet been adequately investigated.

26. THE INSTINCT TO WORK

Before these new discoveries were made, the laws governing the psychic growth of children were absolutely unknown. But now it seems likely that the study of the "sensitive periods" may constitute one of the most important sciences dealing with man.

Growth and development depend upon a continued narrowing of the relationships between a child and his environment. The reason for this is that the development of his personality, or what is called his "freedom," cannot take place unless he becomes progressively independent of adults. And this growth is effected by means of a suitable environment, in which a child can find the necessary means for the development of his own proper functions. A parallel to this may be found in the weaning of infants. Food is prepared for them from cereals that will be a substitute for their mother's milk. In other words, they no longer draw their nourishment from their mothers but from the products of their environment.

It would be a mistake to speak about a child's progressive attainment of freedom without at the same time furnishing him with the kind of environment that will enable him to become independent. The preparation of such surroundings, however, like the proper feeding of children, demands close study. Nevertheless, the basic outline of a new system of education that will properly take care of a child's psychic needs has been drawn by children themselves. And this outline is clear enough to be followed and put into practice.

The most important discovery is that a child returns to a normal state through work. Countless experiments made upon children of every race throughout the world have shown that this is the most certain datum that we have in the field of psychology and education. A child's desire to work represents a vital instinct since he cannot organize his personality without working: *a man builds himself through working.* There can be no substitute for work, neither affection nor physical well-being can replace it. And on the other hand, if this instinct to work becomes diverted, there is no remedy for it either in the example of others or in punishments. A man builds himself by carrying out manual labor in which he uses his hands as the instruments of his personality and as an expression of his intellect and will, helping him to dominate his environment. A child's instinct for work is a proof that work is instinctive to man and characteristic of the species.

Why then has work, which should be a source of great satisfaction and a principle of health and regeneration (as it is for children), been rejected by adults who simply regard it as a harsh necessity? It may be due to the fact that society has lost the proper motives for work. The profound instinct for work remains hidden within man as a recessive trait: it has been deviated by a desire for possessions, for power, and by apathy and attachment. Amid such conditions work depends solely on external circumstances or is occasioned by the mutual struggles of deviated men. It thus becomes forced labor which in turn gives rise to powerful psychic barriers. And this is why work seems hard and repugnant.

But when because of favorable circumstances work flows naturally from an inner impulse, it assumes an entirely different character, even in adults. When this happens, work becomes fascinating and irresistible and raises a man above his diverted self. Examples of this may be found in the toils of an inventor, the discoveries of explorers, and the paintings of artists. When a man is engaged in such war, he becomes possessed of an extraordinary power and experiences again that natural instinct that enables him to express his own individuality. This instinct is like a powerful stream that gushes forth from the earth and provides refreshment for mankind. It is the source of true progress in civilization, for men have a natural instinct for work, and it is through work that their environment is perfected. Work is characteristic of men, and progress in civilization is directly linked with their manifold ability to create an environment that will make life more easy and comfortable.

In such an environment men thrust aside a natural way of living. Nevertheless the new environment which they create cannot be called artificial. Since it transcends rather than replaces nature, it may perhaps be best described as transcendent. Men become progressively so habituated to this transcendent order that it becomes their vital element.

In natural history we notice a process of slow evolution that results in the production of a new species. An example of this may be found in the passage of animals from a maritime to a terrestrial form of life through the amphibia. Somewhat similarly, man began with a natural life and has gradually created for himself a transcendent environment. Man today no longer lives simply according to nature, but nonetheless he makes full use of both the visible and invisible forces of nature.

Man has not simply passed from one vital environment to another: he has constructed for himself his new environment and is now so dependent upon it that he could not live apart from his marvelous creation. Man's life therefore depends upon other men. Nature does not assist him as it does other living creatures. A bird finds its food ready for the eating and materials with which to build its nest, but man has to obtain from other men what he needs. We are all dependent upon each other, and each one of us contributes through his own labors to that transcendent environment in which we all must live.

But if man is dependent upon other men, he is at least the master of his own existence and able to direct and dispose of it as he pleases. He is not immediately subject to the vicissitudes of nature. He is isolated from them and depends exclusively upon human vicissitudes, and his whole life will be in danger if the personalities of those about him have been warped.

The intimate connection between work and the attainment of normality is the best proof of the fact that a man has a natural instinct for work. Nature urges him on to build something by himself that will be an expression of his own existence and further the ends of creation itself. Indeed, it would be unreasonable to think that man does not share in the harmony of the universe to which all living beings contribute, each according to the instincts of its particular species. Corals construct islands and continents by rebuilding the coasts worn away by the ceaseless action of the waves. Insects carry pollen from one blossom to another and thus enable plants to propagate themselves. Vultures and hyenas are scavengers that cleanse the earth of unburied bodies. Some animals rid the world of waste materials and others produce such useful things as honey, wax, silk, and so forth.

Living beings surround the earth almost like the atmosphere, and individual living things are dependent upon others for the preservation of life on earth. Indeed, the life that covers the earth is regarded today as a *biosphere*. Living creatures do not simply preserve themselves in existence and provide for the preservation of their species, but they all work together in a kind of terrestrial harmony. Animals produce more than they actually need for themselves. This results in a surplus that far surpasses the immediate needs of conservation. They may therefore be regarded as workers in the universe and the followers of natural laws. Man, the worker par excellence, must also fall within these general laws. He builds for himself a transcendent environment which, because of the richness of its production, obviously surpasses the simple fact of existence and pertains rather to a cosmic order.

The perfection of man's works is not to be measured by man's own personal needs but by the mysterious designs of his instinct to work. By a fatal deviation man has been separated from his goal in life. If a child is to become the kind of a man that he should, his development must be intimately united with his own guiding instinct. The normal education of a child should thus lead to man's transcendence.

27. TWO DIFFERENT KINDS OF WORK

Although child and adult are made to love each other and to live together in harmony, they are constantly at odds because of the failure to understand each other, which gnaws at the roots of their existence.

This conflict gives rise to many different problems. Some of these are obvious and are connected with their mutual relationships. An adult has a complicated and intense mission to fulfill in life. It becomes increasingly more difficult for him to interrupt his own labors to satisfy the needs of a child by adapting himself to the latter's rhythms and psychic outlook. And, on the other hand, the ever increasing complexity and intensity of an adult's world is not attuned to a child. In contrast with the artificial character of contemporary civilization, we can call to mind the simple, peaceful lives of primitive peoples, where a child could find a natural refuge. In such societies a child came in contact with adults engaged in simple work carried out in a peaceful, tranquil manner. The child was surrounded by domestic animals and other objects which he could freely touch. He could do his own work without fear of protest. When he felt tired, he simply lay down beneath a shady tree and went to sleep.

But civilization has slowly withdrawn the natural environment from the child. Everything is regulated, rapid, and confined. Not only has the accelerated rhythm of adult life proved to be an obstacle to the child, but the advent of machines has swept away his last places of refuge like a whirlwind. A child can no longer engage in the natural activities that he should. The care lavished upon him is largely concerned with protecting him from the perils of existence, which are constantly being multiplied to the increased detriment of the child. He is now like an exile in the world, helpless and enslaved. No one thinks of creating for him a suitable environment or reflects on the need which he has of work and activity.

Since there are two forms of life, that of the child and that of the adult, we must be convinced that there are two distinct social problems and two essentially different types of work.

THE WORK OF THE ADULT

An adult has his own task to perform, that of building up a transcendent environment. He must use his intelligence and external efforts for productive work, which is as a rule both social and collective.

In carrying out his work a man must follow the norms of organized society. These laws must be voluntarily followed to obtain the common goal. But in addition to these laws which are demanded by local customs and which are the source of different cultures, there are other laws pertaining to work rooted in nature itself. Laws of this kind are common to all men and to all times. One of the laws found among all living beings is that of the division of labor. Among men it is indispensable since they cannot all produce the same things. There is another natural law that has reference to an individual's own work. This is the law of minimum effort, according to which one seeks to attain the maximum productivity with the least expenditure of energy. This is a law of utmost importance. It represents not so much a desire to do as little work as possible as to produce as much as one can with the least effort. It is a principle applied to machines that complement man's own labors.

All of these laws are good, even if they are not always universally applicable. Since the material resources at a man's disposal are limited, his desire to enrich himself engenders competition. A struggle for life like that found among brute beasts consequently ensues.

In addition to these natural conflicts there are others caused by deviations in individuals. Among these may be listed the longing for possessions without reference to the preservation of the individual or of the species. Since this longing has no natural origin, it is unlimited. Another deviation is possessiveness, which dominates love, replacing it with hatred. When this enters an organized environment, it is an obstacle not only to individual but also to corporate work. Exploitation of the work of others thus takes the place of the natural division of labor. The guiding norm becomes convenience which, under the guise of rights, establishes the results of human deviations as social principles. In this way error triumphs and is taken as a part of human life and morality. Under a tragic cloud that is not recognized as such everything becomes warped, and all accept as inevitable the consequent ills.

A child is a natural being living in the midst of adults. He finds himself in an alien atmosphere. He has nothing to do with the social activities of adults. His own activities have nothing to do with the production of things that would be useful to society. We must be firmly convinced of the fact that a child simply cannot participate in the social activities of adults. If we would represent man's labor as that of a smith striking an anvil with a heavy hammer, it would be perfectly obvious that a child could not engage in it. If we would represent intellectual toil as that of a scientist using delicate instruments in a difficult research project, it would be equally clear that a child could have nothing to contribute to it. Or we might even think of a legislator drawing up new laws: a child could never replace him in such a task.

A child is completely foreign to this organized society of adults. His "kingdom" is certainly "not of this world." He is a stranger to that artificial world which men have built above nature. A child comes into the world as an asocial being since he cannot adapt himself to society nor contribute to its productivity nor influence its structure. He is rather a disturber of the accepted order. A child is asocial in that he is a source of disturbance wherever there are adults, even in his own home. His lack of adaptation to an adult environment is aggravated by the fact that he is naturally active and constitutionally incapable of renouncing this activity.

Adults are inclined to repress a child's activity. Since they do not want to be disturbed or annoyed, they attempt to make the child passive. A child is confined to a nursery or even to a school. He is condemned by adults to these places of exile until he reaches an age when he can live in an adult world without causing others distress. It is only then that a child is admitted to society. Prior to this he has to obey adults like a person deprived of civil rights. A child has an adult as his lord and master and must always be subject to his bidding, from which there is no appeal.

A child must start from nothing and make his way into the company of adults. In comparison with the child an adult is great and powerful like a god, and it is from him that the child must obtain the necessities of life. The adult is the child's creator, ruler, guardian, and benefactor. Never is anyone so utterly dependent upon another as a child is upon an adult.

THE WORK OF THE CHILD

A child is also a worker and a producer. Although he cannot share in the work of adults, he has its own difficult and important task to perform, that of producing a man. The newborn child is helpless and incapable of moving about. But this tiny child eventually grows into an adult, and if the latter's intelligence has become enriched through his psychic conquests and become resplendent with a spiritual light, this is due to the child that he once was.

It is solely from a child that a man is formed. An adult cannot take part in this labor. An adult is more definitely excluded from a child's world than the child himself is from the transcendent social world of the adult. A child's labor is far different from and, we might say, even opposed to that of an adult. It is an unconscious labor brought about by a spiritual energy in the process of developing. It is a creative labor which recalls the biblical description of man being created. But how was man created? How did man receive intelligence and power over all creation even though he came from nothing? We can observe and admit this wondrous event in all its details in any and every child. Every day our eyes contemplate this marvelous spectacle.

What happened at man's first creation is reproduced in all men when they come into the land of the living. We can thus constantly repeat, "The child is the father of the man." All the powers of the adult flow from the potentialities which the child has of fulfilling the secret mission entrusted to him. What makes a child a real worker is the fact that he does not develop into a man simply by rest and reflection. Rather he is engaged in active work. He creates by constant labor, and we must remember that for this labor he uses the same external environment which the adult uses and transforms. A child grows through exercise. His constructive efforts constitute a real work which takes place in an external environment.

A child gains experience through exercise and movement. He coordinates his own movements and records the emotions he experiences in coming into contact with the external world. These help to mold his intelligence. He laboriously learns how to speak by listening attentively and making those initial efforts which are possible for him alone, and with tireless efforts he succeeds in learning how to stand erect and run about. As the child grows he follows a schedule as closely as any earnest student, with that same invariable constancy with which the stars move along their invisible courses. In fact, we can measure the height of a child at every stage of his development and he will reach the foreseen limits. We also know that he will come to one level of intelligence at five and another at eight. Since a child will obey the plan fixed for him by nature, we can also foresee what his height will be, and his intellectual capacity, at ten. By means of his constant efforts, experiences, sorrows, and conquests of difficult trials and struggles, a child slowly perfects his activities. An adult can assist in shaping the environment, but it is the child that perfects his own being. He is like a man who is always running so that he can attain his goal. The perfections of an adult are thus dependent upon his efforts as a child.

We adults are dependent upon the child. With respect to his sphere of activity, we are his sons and dependents, just as he is our son and dependent in our particular sphere of work. The adult is master in one area, but the child is master in the other, and the two depend upon each other. Both child and adult are kings, but they are rulers of different realms.

A COMPARISON OF THE TWO TYPES OF WORK

Since a child's work consists in actions upon real objects in the external world, they can be made the object of a special study. After the origins and modes of his operations have been investigated, they can be compared with those of adults. Both child and adult carry on an immediate, conscious, and voluntary action upon their environment that may be regarded as work in the proper sense of the term. But here the comparison ends since they each have a different goal to achieve which is not directly known and willed. All life, even that of plants, develops at the expense of its environment. But life itself is an energy that tends to keep the balance of creation by constantly perfecting the environment without which this energy would itself disintegrate. Coral polyps, for example, draw calcium carbonate from the waters of the sea so that they can build their protective coverings. This is the specific goal of their activity, but in the general plan of creation they also build up new continents. Since this ultimate goal is far removed from their immediate activity, we can learn a great deal about corals and coral reefs without ever taking up the question of new continents. The same could be said of all living beings and especially of men.

The fact that every adult is the product of the creative activity of a child proves that the child has a definite, visible, and ultimate goal. Nevertheless we could study a child from every angle and know everything about him from the cells of his body to the smallest details of his countless operations and we would still not perceive his ultimate goal, that is, the adult he is to become.

And yet, the two remote goals of a single act imply work at the expense of the environment.

Nature can at times use simple means to reveal some portion of her secrets. Among insects, for example, we may note the effects of truly productive labor. One of these is silk, the brilliant thread which men weave into precious fabrics. The other is the spider's web made up of fragile threads which men hasten to destroy. And yet, silk is a product of the silkworm a being that is still maturing, whereas the web is the product of an adult spider. This comparison should help us to realize that when we speak of the work of a child and compare it with that of an adult, we are speaking of two real activities but distinct in kind and goal.

It is important for us to know the nature of a child's work. When a child works, he does not do so to attain some further goal. His objective in working is the work itself, and when he has repeated an exercise and brought his own activities to an end, this end is independent of external factors. As far as the child's personal reactions are concerned, his cessation from work is not connected with weariness since it is characteristic of a child to leave his work completely refreshed and full of energy.

This illustrates one of the fundamental differences between the natural laws of work for children and for adults. A child does not follow the law of minimum effort, but rather the very opposite. He consumes a great deal of energy in working for no ulterior end and employs all his potentialities in the execution of each detail. The external object and action are in every case of only accidental importance. There is a striking relationship between the environment and the perfecting of a child's inner life. A man who achieves sublimation is not preoccupied with external things. He only uses them at the proper time for the perfecting of his own inner life. In contrast to such a man, one who is leading an ordinary life is preoccupied with some external goals and he persues them at any cost, sometimes to the extent of losing his health or even his soul.

Another obvious difference between the work of an adult and that of a child lies in the fact that a child does not look for gain or assistance. A child must carry out his work by himself and he must bring it to completion. No one can bear a child's burden and grow up in his stead. Nor is it possible for a child to speed up the rate of his development. One of the special characteristics of a growing being is that it must follow a kind of schedule that does not admit delays or accelerations. Nature is strict and punishes the least acts of disobedience with functional deviations, that is, with abnormalities or ills known as "retardations."

A child possesses a driving force that is different from that of an adult. The adult always acts for some external motive that demands his strenuous efforts and arduous sacrifices. But if a man is to carry out this mission, he must have received the strength and courage to do so from the child that he was.

A child, on the other hand, does not become weary with toil. He grows by working and, as a consequence, his work increases his energy. A child never asks to be relieved of his burdens but simply that he may carry out his mission completely and alone. His very life consists in the work of growth since he must work or die.

If adults do not understand this secret they will never understand the work of children any more than they have understood it in the past. They place obstacles in the way of a child's work, thinking that rest will be of greater assistance to his proper growth. An adult does everything for the child instead of letting the child act as he should. An adult is interested in using the least effort and in saving time. Since adults are more experienced and agile, they seek to wash and clothe a child and carry him about in their arms or in a buggy and to rearrange a child's room without letting him help.

When a child is given a little leeway, he will at once shout, "I want to do it!" But in our schools, which have an environment adapted to children's needs, they say, "Help me to do it alone." And these words reveal their inner needs.

What a profound truth lies behind this paradox! An adult must assist a child in such a way that he can act and carry out his own work in the world. This reveals not only the child's need but also the fact that he should be surrounded by a vital environment. Such an environment is not one for the child to conquer and enjoy but a means that will enable him to perfect his various activities. This environment must obviously be prepared by an adult who knows a child's inner needs. Our concept of the education of children thus differs not only from those who do everything for a child themselves but also from those who think that they can leave the child in a purely passive environment.

It is therefore not enough to prepare objects for children adapted in size and shape to their needs: adults must also be trained to help them.

28. THE GUIDING INSTINCTS

There are two forms of life in nature: one that is mature and another that is still immature. These two types are quite diverse and even opposed to each other. The life of adults is characterized by struggle. These conflicts may have their origin in adaptation to an environment, as illustrated by Lamarck, or they may have their source in competition and natural selection, as illustrated by Darwin. Conflicts of the latter type not only further the survival of the species, but they lead to natural selection through sexual conquest.

The growth of society may be compared with what happens among grown animals. Men must exert constant efforts to preserve their lives and defend themselves from their enemies; they encounter toil and trouble as they adapt themselves to their environment, and they are moved to love and sexual conquest. Darwin traced the cause of evolution, that is, the gradual perfecting of living beings and the survival of the fittest to these forces and rivalries among the species. In a similar fashion materialistic historians attribute the evolution of humanity to the contests and rivalries among men.

The only sources that we have at our disposal for the writing of human history are the various activities of adults. But this is not so in nature. Here the real key to the understanding of life in its countless, marvelous manifestations is the young and growing being. All living beings are too weak at first to struggle, and all begin to exist before they have any organs to adapt. No living being begins its life as an adult.

There must then be a hidden kind of life with another

form, other means, and other incentives different from those that appear in the interplay between mature individuals and their environment. A study of creatures in the process of development is of utmost importance since the true key of life is to be found in them. The experiences of adults only explain the accidents of survival.

Biologists who have studied the infant life of creatures have thrown light on the most wonderful and complex part of nature. They have shown that the whole of living creation is filled with astounding wonders and sublime potentialities. All nature, in a word, is replete with poetry. Biology has shown how species preserve themselves through impulses that act as inner guides. These may be called "guiding instincts" to distinguish them from the immediate instictive reactions of a being to its environment.

Biologically, all instincts may be divided into two fundamental classes according to their separate goals, that is, whether they pertain to the preservation of the individual or to that of the species. In both classes may be found transient and permanent reactions or attitudes. There are, for example, passing conflicts between an individual and its particular surroundings, and there are other fixed and guiding instincts necessary for the preservation of the life of the individual.

Among the transient instinct pertaining to the preservation of the individual, for example, is the defense it raises against whatever is hostile or threatening. Among the instincts, on the other hand, that pertain to the preservation of the species, there is the transient reaction that leads to sexual conflict or union. These episodic instincts, since they are more violent and apparent, were the first observed and studied by biologists. Later, however, more attention was paid to the instincts connected with the preservation of the individual and the species that are of a more permanent character. These have been defined as the guiding instincts.

The very existence of life itself in its cosmic functions is connected with these instincts. They are not so much reactions to an environment as delicate inner sensibilities, just as pure thought is an inner quality of the mind. They may be considered as the divine thoughts being elaborated within the intimacy of the living being to assist it in its operations upon the outer world. The guiding instincts, therefore, do not have the impulsive character of passing conflicts but are marked by a knowledge and wisdom that guides these beings in their voyage through time (the individuals) and in eternity (the species).

The guiding instincts are a cause of special wonder in the direction and protection they afford an infant at the very beginning of its life, when it is still very immature but on the way to attaining its full development, when it does not as yet have the special characteristics of the species, nor the strength, nor the endurance, nor the biological weapons for the contest, nor even the hope of final victory, whose reward is survival. Here the guiding instincts act like a mother or pedagogue hidden within the secret of creation. They save the helpless creature that has neither the strength nor the means to save itself.

One of these guiding instincts is connected with maternity. It has been shown by Fabre and other biologists to be a kind of key to the survival of a species. Another has reference to the growth of the individual and has been described by the Dutch scholar De Vries in his research on the sensitive periods.

The maternal instinct is not confined solely to females, although they are the procreatrices of the species and play the greatest part in protecting the young, but it is found in both parents and at times pervades a whole group. A more profound study of this maternal instinct reveals that it is a mysterious energy which is not necessarily connected with existing individuals but which exists for the protection of the species.

"Maternal instinct" is thus a generic definition given to the guiding instinct that is concerned with the preservation of the species. It has certain characteristics that are common to all living creatures. For one thing, it demands a sacrifice of all other adult instincts. A fierce animal can show a tenderness and gentleness that is not natural to it. A bird which flies far in search of food or to save itself from danger will closely watch its nest. It will find other means of fending off dangers, but never that of flight. Instincts that are inherent in a species unexpectedly change their character. Many species will work to build a place of refuge. This tendency is not found in them at other times, for once they are fully grown they simply adapt themselves to nature as they find it. Their building activities are directed to preparing a shelter for their young. And each species has its own plan to follow. No living being gathers at random the first material that it encounters or simply adapts itself to a particular locality. No, the instructions given in this regard by its maternal instinct are fixed and precise.

The way in which a bird builds its nest is one means of identifying the species to which it belongs. Insects are marvelous builders. Beehives are, for example, veritable palaces built upon perfect geometrical lines. The whole hive works together to build this home for the next generation. Other examples of industry, less spectacular but extremely interesting, could also be noted. There is the spider that stretches her large nets for her foes. But then all of a sudden she forgets her foes and her own needs and undertakes a radically new type of work. She fashions a tiny sack of fine, densely woven threads. This is waterproof and frequently made in two layers to resist the cold and damp of a spider's normal habitat. Within the pouch the spider lays her eggs, but the remarkable fact is that the spider is so strongly attached to this sack that she can die of grief at the distressing sight of her sack being torn or destroyed. She is, in fact, so closely attached to her pouch that it seems to be a part of her body. Her affection, therefore, is centered on the sack but not upon the eggs nor the tiny spiders that finally emerge from them. It seems as if she does not even notice their existence. Instinct has led this mother to do something for the species without her having a living being as a direct object. There can thus be an instinct without an existing object which acts irresistibly and represents submission to an inner command to do what is necessary and to love what has been commanded.

There are butterflies which during the whole of their lives feed on the nectar of flowers without craving any other food. But when the time comes for them to lay their eggs they never deposit them on flowers. They are guided by another instinct. The instinct for food which is directed toward the good of the individual is replaced by another. The butterflies turn towards a different kind of food, one which is of no use to them themselves but which is necessary for the larvae from which the butterflies eventually emerge. Insects thus bear within themselves commands of nature that are foreign to their own being but which are for the good of the species. Ladybugs and similar insects never place their eggs on the top, but on their lower sides of leaves, where the larvae that will come out of the eggs and feed upon the leaves will be protected. Similar instincts are found in numerous other insects which never feed upon the plants they choose for the sustenance of their offspring. They instinctively know what will be the proper nourishment of their young and even foresee the dangers that may come from rain and sun.

A creature which has the mission of preserving the species changes its own inclinations and transforms itself as if the laws governing its own life had been for a time suspended and it stood in expectation of some great natural event—the miracle of creation. It then transcends its usual activities and performs what could be described as a rite in the presence of this miracle.

And, in fact, one of the most resplendent miracles of nature is the power which the newborn have, despite their utter lack of experience, to orientate themselves within, and to protect themselves from, the external world. They are able to do this with the help of the partial instincts of their sensitive periods. These instincts are the guides that lead them through successive difficulties and animate them from time to time with irresistible drives. Nature has not given to adults the same protection that it has to the newly born. She has her own norms and watches carefully to see that they are obeyed. Adults must simply collaborate within the limits established by the guiding instincts for the protection of the species.

Frequently, as may be seen in the case of fish and insects, the guiding instincts of the adult and of the new-born creature act in a distinct and independent manner. When this happens, parents and offspring never associate with each other. In higher animals the two instincts work harmoniously together and the concurrence of the guiding instincts of the mother with the sensitive period of her offspring begets a reciprocal love between mother and child, or a maternal relationship is established that extends to the whole of an organized society which takes over the care of the new generation. This occurs, for example, among insects living in communities, such as bees, ants, and so forth.

The species is not protected by love and sacrifice. Rather these are the effects of the guiding instinct which, having its roots in the great creative laboratory of life, determines the survival of every species. The emotion or sentiment which creatures have in caring for their offspring facilitates the task imposed by nature and affords that special pleasure which is found in a perfect obedience to nature's bidding.

If we would wish to embrace the adult world in a single glance, we could say that exceptions are periodically made to the laws governing it. The natural laws, which seem to be so absolute and unchangeable, are suspended for a higher good. They yield to the demands of new laws that favor the infant life of the species. Thus, by a constant suspension and renovation of nature's laws, life is perpetually maintained.

We may now ask ourselves how man fits into these laws of nature. Man is the ultimate synthesis containing within himself all the natural phenomena of lesser beings. He epitomizes and surpasses them and, what is more, through his intelligence he clothes them in a rational splendor that is manifested in his works of art.

How, then, are these two forms of life, that is, of child and adult represented in man, and under what sublime aspects do they reveal themselves? Actually these two lives are not apparent. If we were to search for them in the world of men, we would have to say that there is only an adult world, one preoccupied with externals and securing an easy existence. Men's minds are concentrated on conquest and production as if there were no other matters of importance. Human effort lashes out and is broken in competition. If an adult looks at the life of a child, he does so with the same logic that he regards his own. He sees a child as a different kind of being and keeps this useless creature far away. Or, with what is regarded as education, he attempts to draw a child directly within the orbit of his own way of life. He acts as a butterfly would act (if it were possible) that would break the cocoon of its larva to encourage it to fly. Or he acts like a frog that would draw its tadpole out of the water so that it might breathe on land, and would change its dark skin into the green with which it is itself clothed.

This is more or less the way in which men act towards their children. Adults show them their own proper perfections, their maturity, their historical examples, and they expect the children to imitate them. They fail to realize that a child's life is such that it needs a different kind of environment and a different means of life.

How can we explain such a great misunderstanding on the part of man, the most evolved, the highest form of being in the material universe, one endowed with his own intelligence, the master of his environment, full of power, and immeasurably superior to other living beings in his ability to work?

And yet man, architect, builder, producer, and molder of his environment does less for his child than the bee and other insects for their young. Is the highest and the most essential of life's guiding instincts completely lacking in man? Is he truly helpless and blind before a staggering phenomenon characteristic of all life which guarantees the very existence of the species?

Man should have feelings like those of other beings, for in nature everything is transformed but nothing destroyed. The forces that pervade the universe survive even if they are turned aside from their proper objects.

Man is a builder, but where does he build a nest suitable for his child? It should be a place of beauty and uncontaiminated by any outward need. It should be a place where a generous love can store up riches not used for production. Is there any place where a man feels the need to abandon his usual mode of acting, where he perceives that struggle is not an essential part of life, where he comes to realize that getting the better of others is not the secret of survival, and where, as a consequence, self-renunciation seems to be a true source of life? Is there no place where a soul longs to break the iron bonds that hold it fast to the world of external things? Is there no anxious looking for a miracle, a miracle that will foster new life? Is there likewise no longing for something that transcends the life of the individual and stretches out towards eternity? This is the way of salvation: man sees that he must give up his own laborious reasonings and come to believe.

These are the sentiments which rise in a man at the birth of his child. Like other living creatures he should give up his own way of acting and make a holocaust of himself so that life may be carried forward towards eternity.

Yes, there are places when a man no longer feels the need of conquest but of purification and innocence, where he longs for simplicity and peace. In that innocent peace man seeks for a renewal of his life, for a kind of resurrection from the burdens of the world.

Yes, there must be in man great aspirations that are far removed from those of ordinary life. They represent a divine voice that nothing can still, calling men together to stand about the child.

29. THE CHILD AS A TEACHER

One of the most important objects for research today is the discovery of man's guiding instincts. With no precedents to guide us, we have opened up this new field of investigation. We have demonstrated the existence of certain instincts and indicated how they can be further studied. But such a study is only possible among normal children, that is, among those who live in an environment that is suitable for proper growth. When this happens, a new human nature is so clearly revealed that there can be no doubt about its normal character.

Countless experiences have brought to light a truth that is of great importance for education and society. It is clear that if men had a nature different from the one we know, they would have a different form of social organization. But if such a normalization of adult society is to be brought about, it must be done through education. A social change of this type cannot come from the ideas or energies of individual reformers but from a slow and steady emergence of a new world in the midst of the old, the gradual appearance of the world of the child and adolescent. From this world should gradually come the revelations and natural guidance that can lead society to a normal life. It is foolish to hope or even to imagine that theoretical reforms or individual efforts could fill so great a void as that which has been made in the world through the oppression of children. As long as children cannot develop according to nature's norms but suffer deviations, men will always be abnormal. The energy that can help mankind is that which lies within the child.

We must insist upon the attainment of the ancient ideal

contained in the saying, "Know thyself!" The various biological sciences that have contributed so much to men's physical well-being have started with this dictum. Though man has made great strides in physical hygiene, his psychic life is still an unknown quantity. The first great advances in the knowledge of the human body were made through the dissecting of cadavers. New advances in the understanding of the human mind will be made through a study of the newborn child. Such studies seem to be necessary for the progress of civilization. The problems of education and of society will remain unsolved as long as there is no basis for their solution, that is, the normalization of the child.

The same might be said of adults. They are confronted with the problem of self-knowledge, that is, of knowledge of the hidden laws that direct the psychic development of man. But this problem has already been resolved by the child in a practical way, and there seems to be no other solution. Deviated men, who seek to obtain power and authority, can become obsessed with any good, which is then transformed into something dangerous before it can be rightly used. This is why any good, any discovery or invention, can increase the ills that afflict the world. We can see this social effect produced by machines. They can be used to further man's material well-being or for war and the heaping up of excessive profits. The progress that has been made in physics, chemistry, and biology, and the discovery of new means of transportation have augmented the danger of increased misery and the eventual triumph of barbarism. We can thus place no hopes in the external world until the normalization of man is recognized as a basic social need. Only then will material progress bring true blessings and a higher form of civilization.

Within the child lies the fate of the future. Whoever wishes to confer some benefit on society must preserve him from deviations and observe his natural ways of acting. A child is mysterious and powerful and contains within himself the secret of human nature.

30. THE RIGHTS OF THE CHILD

Up until the turn of the century society was not at all concerned with the child. It was left exclusively in the care of the family. The only protection that he had was his father's authority, a relic of Roman law going back some two thousand years. During this long period of time advances were made in civilization and many improvements were made in the laws for adults. But children were left deprived of any such defense. A child received the material, moral, and intellectual assistance which the family into which he was born could afford. If a child's family was without resources, society felt no responsibility in his regard, and he grew up in the midst of material, moral, and intellectual misery. Society did not ask husband and wife to prepare themselves so that they could take proper care of their children. The state, which was so rigorous in the drawing up of official documents, so meticulous with the smallest formalities, and so anxious to regulate every other aspect of society, was not in the least concerned about the ability of future parents to protect their children and provide for their proper development. Nor did it give any kind of preparation or instruction that would have helped these parents to assume their responsibilities. Even now all that a man and woman need to do to establish a family is to obtain a license and go through the marriage ceremony.

From all this we may conclude that society has long been indifferent to the tiny workers to whom nature has entrusted the role of the building of humanity. In contrast with the constant benefits that have been heaped upon adults, children have remained exiled and forgotten.

It was only about seventy years ago that physicians began to take a real interest in children and began to realize that they were the victims of society. At that time children were even more abandoned than they are today. There were no specialists or hospitals set aside for children. But when statistical studies revealed the high incidence of infant mortality, men were aroused from their lethargy. The figures showed that, even though many children might be born into a family, only a relatively few survived. The death of small children seemed so natural that families consoled themselves with the thought that their offspring passed immediately to heaven. So many infants died through ignorance and lack of care that their deaths were considered to be quite normal.

But when men came to realize that something could be done for these children, an extensive campaign was undertaken to stir up the consciences of their parents. They were told that it was not enough for them to give life to their children but that they should also use the new discoveries of science to save them from sickness and death. This meant that they would have to learn the principles of child hygiene and apply them.

But it was not only within the bosom of their family that children suffered. In the last decade of the nineteenth century, when physicians were studying diseases among workers and laying the foundations for social hygiene, it was discovered that, in addition to the infectious diseases that resulted from a lack of hygiene, children were also afflicted with other ills.

They had to undergo sufferings in school imposed upon them by society. Bending for long hours over a desk while learning how to read and write caused a constriction of the spinal column and a narrowing of the chest that predisposed these children to tuberculosis. Prolonged effort to read without sufficient light caused nearsightedness, and their bodies were in general weakened through long confinement in narrow, crowded quarters.

But their sufferings were not simply of a physical nature; they were spiritual as well. Forced study brought on fear, weariness, and nervous exhaustion. They became disheartened, and melancholy replaced their natural gaiety.

Families, as a rule, took little account of all this. The parents of a child were solely interested in seeing a child pass his examinations and learning as quickly as possible so that there would be no further expenditures for education. They were not much concerned with learning for its own sake or with cultural attainments. They were simply attending to an expensive social obligation. All that interested them was that a child should acquire a social passport in the least possible time.

Investigations made at the time revealed some interesting facts. Many children came to school wearied from tasks they had already performed. Some had walked for several miles before school distributing milk to customers, others had sold newspapers on the streets or had worked at home. They thus came to school tired and hungry. Nonetheless these same children were frequently punished for being inattentive and failing to understand the teacher. The latter, concerned with his reponsibilities and still more with his authority, sought to awaken their interest by scolding them. He exacted obedience with threats or humiliated his charges in the presence of their companions by reproaching them with their lack of ability or weakness of will. Children thus spent their lives being exploited at home and punished in school.

So much injustice was revealed by these early investigations that a reaction set in. Various changes were made in schools. Doctors and teachers now worked together for the health of the students. The introduction of these school health programs has had a beneficial influence in all civilized countries. They mark the first step towards the social redemption of childhood.

If we look back beyond this first saluatory awakening we shall not find in the whole course of history any evidence of a recognition of the rights of a child, or any appreciation of their importance. And yet Christ, to arouse men from their blindness and to point out to them the way to the Kingdom of Heaven, had embraced a child and said, "If you do not become as one of these little children, you shall not enter into the Kingdom of Heaven." But despite this salutary warning adults continued to be preoccupied with bringing a child to their own way of living, setting themselves up as examples for his perfection. And it seemed as if their tremendous blindness was wholly incurable. This universal blindness, old as humanity itself, is certainly one of the great mysteries of the human soul.

From remote antiquity down to our own days education has been synonymous with punishment. The end of education was to subject the child to an adult, who substituted himself for nature and replaced the laws of life with his own desires and intents. Support for this attitude was found in the Book of Proverbs where a father could read that if he spared the rod he would spoil the child. During the course of thousands of years, no great changes have been made. People of different nations have used different means for punishing children. In private schools there frequently are fixed modes of punishment. These may include the hanging of a humiliating sign about a child's neck, putting the ears of an ass on his head, or exposing him to the insults and derision of anyone who happens to pass by. There are other punishments that entail physical pain. Among these are forcing a child to stand for hours with his face towards a corner, or to kneel on the floor with bare knees, or to be whipped in public. A modern refinement of cruelty has sprung from the theoretical union of family and school in the work of education. The child who has been punished in school is obliged to reveal the fact at home so that his father may add his own reproaches and chastisements to those of the teacher. The child is then compelled to bring a note from his father to show that he has been informed of his son's misdeeds.

In such cases a child finds it impossible to defend himself. To what tribunal can he turn? He does not even have the right of appeal enjoyed by a condemned criminal. And where is the love that might serve a child as a consoling refuge in his troubles? There is none. Teachers and family unite in inflicting punishment upon a child in the belief that otherwise the correction would be ineffective. But families do not need to be reminded that they should punish their children. Studies of the various ways in which children are punished show that even in our own day there are no nations in which children are not punished within the family. They are insulted, scolded, slapped, beaten, banished to dark rooms, threatened with even greater punishments, and deprived of the little amusements and recreations, like that of playing with other children or eating candy or fruit, which constitute their sole refuge and the only compensation for so many sufferings unconsciously endured. Then, too, they are forced to go to bed without their supper and thus pass a troubled night because of their grief and hunger.

Although the use of such punishments is rapidly disappearing among educated people, they have not entirely disappeared. Parents still shout at their children in harsh and threatening tones. Adults think they have a natural right to punish a child, and a mother thinks a slap is a duty.

And yet corporal punishment has been abolished for adults as an insult to human dignity and a social disgrace. But is there anything so mean as to insult and beat a child? Man's conscience in this regard has certainly been dulled.

Progress in civilization no longer depends upon individual efforts or the burning flame of the human soul. Its advance is like that of an insensible machine. The driving force is the enormous impersonal power of society moving relentlessly ahead.

Society is like an enormous train traveling at a dizzy speed towards some distant goal, and the individuals who make up this society may be compared with travelers asleep in their compartments. Their sleeping consciences are the greatest obstacle to true progress. If this were not so, there would not be the dangerous contrast between the ever increasing speed of the means of transportation and the ever greater rigidity of the human soul. The first and most difficult step towards social reform is to arouse this slumbering humanity and force it to listen to the voice that is calling. Today it is absolutely necessary that society should become aware of the child and earnestly strive to draw him from the great and perilous abyss in which he lies. The social rights of children must be recognized so that a world suited to their needs may be constructed for them. The greatest crime that society commits is that of wasting the money which it should use for children on things that will destroy them and society itself as well.

Society is like the guardian of a child who has squandered his patrimony. Adults spend money on themselves and build what they want, when it is obvious that a great share of their wealth should be destined for their children. This truth is instinctive in life itself and may be found even in the lowest insects. Why do ants store up provisions? Why do birds seek for food and carry it to their nests? Nature furnishes no examples of adults who devour everything themselves and abandon their own offspring to misery. And yet nothing is done for the child. His body is kept alive and that is all. When, because of its wastefulness, society has an urgent need of money, it takes this from schools, and especially from the lower schools that shelter the seeds of life. It takes it from these schools since there are no voices to defend them. This is one of humanity's worst crimes and errors. Society does not even perceive that it causes double destruction when it uses this money to build instruments of war. It destroys by preventing life and bringing death, but the two are the result of a single error. Since no effort was made to secure their proper development in life, men have grown up in an abnormal manner. Adults must therefore be organized, not for themselves, but for their children. They must raise their voices in the name of a right which their habitual blindness prevents them from seeing but which, if it is once affirmed, could never be questioned. If society has been a faithless guardian of children, it must now set things aright and return to them their inheritance.

THE MISSION OF PARENTS

A child's parents are not his makers but his guardians. They must protect him and have a deep concern for him like one who assumes some scared trust. For their exalted mission, a child's parents should purify the love that nature has implanted in their hearts and they should strive to understand that this love is the conscious expression of a deeper sentiment that should not be contaminated by self-interest or sloth. Parents should be concerned with the great social question of the day, the struggle to gain a recognition of the rights of childhood in the world.

Much has been said in recent years of the rights of man and especially of the rights of workers, but it is now time to speak of the social rights of the child. A recognition of the rights of workers is a matter of fundamental importance for society since it is solely by human toil that humanity survives. But if workers produce what men consume and are the creators of countless objects, the child produces humanity itself and consequently his rights have still greater need of recognition. It is evident that society should lavish upon children the greatest care so that it may in turn receive from the child new energies and potentialities.

Men's consciences should be strongly moved by the fact that they have neglected and forgotten the rights of the child, that they have failed to recognize his worth, his power, and his very nature.

Parents have a very important mission. They are the only ones who can save their children by uniting and working together for the improvement of society. They must come to appreciate the mission which nature has entrusted to them. They have a primary role in society and control the future of humanity in so far as they give life to their children. If they do not act as they should, they will be like Pilate.

Pilate could have saved Christ but he did not do so. A mob held in the grip of ancient prejudices demanded the life of the Redeemer, and Pilate did not effectively oppose them.

Parents today act like Pilate. They abandon their children to social customs as if they were inevitable. No voice is raised in their defense, and yet if there is a voice that should defend them, it is that of love and the power of love, the human authority of their parents.

As Emerson has observed a child is like the Messias in that he descends to fallen men in order to lead them back to the Kingdom of Heaven.

ABOUT THE AUTHOR

MARIA MONTESSORI was born at Chiara-velle, Italy, on August 31, 1870. In 1894 she was the first woman to graduate in Medicine from the University of Rome, and in 1899 she began a study of educational problems of handicapped children. Working on lines first laid down by the French physician E. Seguin, she achieved startling results and the children under her tutelage passed the state examination in reading and writing for normal children. Dr. Montessori concluded that similar methods might also be successfully applied to younger normal children and she began to work with toddlers in private and public schools in Rome. She encountered opposition from advocates of orthodox methods of education who regarded her system, which encouraged freedom of movement, as destructive of discipline, but she was warmly supported by enthusiastic reformers. From 1900 to 1907 Maria Montessori lectured on pedagogical anthropology at the University of Rome and in 1922 she was appointed government inspector of schools in Italy. She wrote more than six books on learning and the child, and the system of education which she developed bears her name. Her later years were spent supervising training courses in Spain, India, England, and the Netherlands. She died at Noordwijk, Netherlands, on May 6, 1952.